Secrets *of* Power
Problem Solving

by

Roger Dawson

CAREER
PRESS
Pompton Plains, NJ

SECRETS OF POWER PROBLEM SOLVING
EDITED BY KATHRYN HENCHES
TYPESET BY EILEEN MUNSON
Cover design by Jeff Piasky
Printed in the U.S.A.

To order this title, please call toll-free 1-800-CAREER-1 (NJ and Canada: 201-848-0310) to order using VISA or MasterCard, or for further information on books from Career Press.

The Career Press, Inc.
220 West Parkway, Unit 12
Pompton Plains, NJ 07444
www.careerpress.com

Library of Congress Cataloging-in-Publication Data
Dawson, Roger, 1940-
  Secrets of power problem solving / by Roger Dawson.
    p. cm.
  Includes index.
  ISBN 978-1-60163-152-7 -- ISBN 978-1-60163-674-4 (ebook) 1. Decision making.
2. Problem solving. I. Title.

  HD30.23.D3737 2011
  153.4'3--dc22

                                                            2011003529

To my beautiful wife, Gisela,

who brought love

back into my life.

To all the attendees of my seminars,

readers of my books,

and listeners to my audio programs

who shared their problem solving stories with me.

To my three astounding children:

Julia, Dwight, and John.

And to my grandchildren:

Astrid and Thomas.

Contents

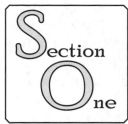

Types of Problems

*If you only have a hammer, you tend to see
every problem as a nail.*

—Abraham Maslow

Ten months a year, I travel the country and a good part of the world, conducting seminars for corporations and associations. This means that I've had a unique opportunity to sit and talk to some of the most successful people in the company. Whenever my schedule permits, I like to have dinner the night before with the president of the company, or the top performer in the association for which I'll be speaking. It's a great opportunity to pick their brains about what made them so successful.

As the topic of problem solving became more and more fascinating to me, I started asking successful businesspeople how they *solved problems.* How do they go about it in their company? What process do they use?

What I found out was fascinating. *Almost nobody has a process for solving problems.* I saw people who had built empires, and were respected by everyone in their industry, and people who could commit millions of dollars to a project and not lose a moment's sleep over it—even they did not seem to know how to solve problems.

A typical response was "A problem comes up, we kick it around, and, if it feels right, we make a move." Isn't that interesting? How much better could they be at what they do, if they just got a little bit better at problem solving?

There is a better way, and the starting point is to change the way you think about problem solving. To become a better problem solver you have to stop focusing on the problem itself, and concentrate on the problem-solving process. With a problem-solving process on which you can rely, you will have the confidence that you're making the right choice, every time.

You may never do the right thing every time, but if you'll learn the simple techniques in this book, you'll be making the right choice all the time.

In Section One, we'll talk about the two major types of problems and how to solve them. Later, I'll teach you the specific steps to great problem solving.

Chapter 1

There Are Only Two Types of Problems

The first step to solving your problem is to decide whether the problem is about money or people. There really are only two different kinds of problems: money problems and people problems. That doesn't sound right to you, does it? It's got to be more complicated than that, you say.

I still remember where I was when I first heard that there are only two kinds of problems. I was living in Bakersfield, California, and somebody suggested that I try attending the Church of Religious Science. When they told me that it wasn't a Christian church I was skeptical. I was raised Church of England (Anglican in the United States), and my first wife was raised Lutheran. Both believe in a strict agenda in church services and sermons taught straight out of the Bible. A church that taught that there are many paths to God and that powerful thinking could change circumstances seemed more like a motivational rally than a religion.

Sitting in this strange environment with my family I was frankly suspicious and looking for reasons to rule Religious Science out of our lives. When the preacher told that us he was going to talk to us about problem solving, it was definitely not the kind of topic that I'd heard from my vicar back home. Then he made the statement that there are only two types of problems—people problems and money problems—and I was convinced that it was sheer baloney. But that was more than 30 years ago and I've never found an exception to that rule.

Don't confuse people problems with money problems

Believe me when I tell you that you'll never find a problem or opportunity that can't be separated this way. Money problems or people problems—there are only two kinds. Or possibly solving the problem will take both money, and people handling skills. People have difficulty solving problems when they confuse the two:

> "I own a chain of 60 two hamburger stands in New Jersey. I started it right out of high school with a thousand bucks I borrowed from my uncle. I built this business with sweat and tears. For three years I worked 18 hours a day seven days a week until I could afford to hire some help. My problem is with that first employee. He's now my executive vice-president. I made this guy. I took him off the street, and now he lives in a mansion and drives a Mercedes. Yesterday, he's got the gall to tell me that he's quitting me and going to work for the competition. How could he do this to me, after all I've done for him? I asked him if he'd stay for more money. He says sure, but he wants fifty thousand more a year! That's blackmail!"

This is an example of a person who really has a money problem, not a people problem. If he could only see this clearly, he'd calm down, and know how to negotiate a solution to the problem. He should be calmly thinking, "Okay, so I can solve this problem for $50,000 a year. But, I know I can do better than that. Fifty thousand is unreasonable and he knows it, so he must be upset about something else. We'll talk, I'll butter him up, and we'll work it out. It's probably not going to cost me anymore than $10K and a new car."

Here's a problem that I hear all the time:

> "My 25-five-year-old son is driving me insane. I
> love him, but I can't stand him living at the house
> anymore. He's driving me crazy with his late-night
> carousing. I've tried laying down ground rules, but
> nothing seems to work. I ought to throw him out
> of the house and let him make his own way in the
> world. It would probably do him a world of good.
> But I hate to break the ties completely. He's my
> only son, and I might never see him again."

This mother thinks she has a people problem when she
really has a money problem. If I asked her how the son would
feel if she gave him $800 a month to rent his own apartment,
she'd tell me: "Well, that would solve everything, but we don't
have the $800 a month to give him." That may be so, but when
I point this out to her, she'll see for the first time that it isn't a
people problem she's facing; it's a money problem.

I know what you're thinking. You're thinking "How shal-
low can one person be? It's not right to think that money can
solve problems involving other people. I don't want to go
through my life buying people off!" I totally agree with you on
that! But if we're going to be great problem solvers we start by
analyzing the situation accurately. Don't confuse people problems with money problems!

➡ Key points from this chapter:

> ▸ There are only two kinds of problems: people
> problems and money problems.

> ▸ People often confuse the two. They think they
> have a people problem when they really have
> only a money problem.

> ▸ Even if it would take a ridiculous amount of
> money to solve the problem, you have a money
> problem, not a people problem.

Chapter 2

Solving People Problems

Now that we know that there are only two types of problems—money problems and people problems—let's take a look at people problems, which are, without a doubt, the more difficult of the two.

Much of what I'm going to teach you here comes from my years of studying hostage situations, which must be the most difficult of all people problems to solve.

Rule one: Don't try to sweep people problems under the rug.

If you've got someone who is mad at you, you might want to back off for 48 hours to see if the problem goes away. Maybe he just lost his temper and now regrets it. Perhaps what he had to say in the heat of the argument now doesn't seem so important and certainly not something over which to jeopardize your relationship.

Learn not to shoot from the hip when someone upsets you. I can't tell you how many times I've stopped myself from an angry response that would have exacerbated the problem. Let the old earth take a couple of whirls, as Frank Sinatra advises in the classic "September Song." Former President Clinton learned that well. As a governor he would get himself into trouble with flip responses like "I never inhaled." As President, and now international ambassador, you can almost hear him counting to 10 with his right thumb extended, before he responds.

But if the other person is still angry with you after 48 hours you need to talk about the problem, not ignore it.

If you've got a boss who is giving you the cold shoulder you need to ask for face-to-face time to discuss the problem. Perhaps he misunderstood your point of view. Maybe another employee has unfairly poisoned your relationship with your boss using unfair accusations.

Perhaps your problem is a parent or child who is being sullen with you over some imagined slight. Don't let it go past 48 hours without addressing the problem.

Rule two: Verify that there really is a problem.

Be careful that you're not overreacting to a situation. The last thing you need is to get a reputation for being so sensitive that people have to watch out for every word they say when they're around you.

If the problem is with your boss you might say to his or her assistant, "Is the boss upset with me? He didn't even speak to me when he came through my department this morning." The response may well be, "Oh no, everything's fine. He's just preoccupied with a hassle he's having with head office."

If the problem is with a child, you might say to her brother or sister "What's bothering your brother these days?"

If you're worried about your parent's reaction to a situation, try, "Mom, what's Dad so upset about these days? He hasn't yelled at me all week!"

Rule three: Keep communications open at all cost.

This is something that I learned from studying hostage negotiations. You have to establish and maintain communications at all cost. Unless you are able to talk to the person the situation is going to get worse.

In a hostage situation the first thing that the negotiators will want to do is establish communications. Figure out a way to get talking with the perpetrators. Don't worry at this stage about how outrageous their demands might be. Get them talking and keep the lines of communication open.

On the opening day of school in Beslan, Russia, a small town between the Caspian and Black Seas, terrorists stormed the facility and took 1,100 parents and children hostage. The authorities correctly isolated the school and attempted to communicate with the perpetrators. "What do you want?" they asked them. "Are you demanding the release of prisoners in Chechen? Do you want money? What is it you want?"

Their reply was, "We don't want anything! We came here to die!" Let me tell you something. That is not a good start to resolving people problems! Unless you can get the other person talking to you, you have little chance of resolving the problem to both sides' satisfaction.

The other thing that went wrong with the Russian school hostage taking was that President Putin took a very strong line. He wanted the negotiations to go no more than three days before he would attack the compound.

There is a thing called acceptance time in a negotiation. It takes time for people to realize that they are not going to accomplish what they want out of the situation. The school hijacking was a situation that demanded a lot of acceptance time. Waiting it out may have taken a few months but it was preferable to what happened when the authorities attacked, costing the lives of 334 people and injuring hundreds.

Rule four: In an impasse create momentum with small concessions.

When neither side sees any possibility of resolving the problem, we call that an impasse in conflict resolution. It's important not to confuse an impasse with a deadlock, which is far more serious.

An impasse is when both sides are so far apart on the major issue that they see no possibility of a peaceful resolution. The way to handle an impasse is to create momentum by reaching agreement on little issues first. It may be that you both agree to keep the issue confidential while you're trying to resolve the problem.

As you create momentum by reaching agreement on little issues, it's important not to narrow the remaining issues too far. If you resolve all the minor issues and are left with only one major issue, there has to be a winner and there has to be a loser.

This is what went wrong when the Iraqis tried to write a constitution for their country. Their first constitution that established a monarchy was created in 1925 under the British occupation. When Iraq became a republic in 1958 they attempted to revise their constitution many times but could not reach agreement. With Saddam's Hussein's dictatorship it all became moot. In 2006, after the U.S. invasion, the new parliament created an Iraqi Constitution Drafting Committee and gave them six months to write a new constitution.

At the end of that time they requested a one-week extension because they still had three issues left to resolve. That sounded encouraging until we asked them to describe the three issues. They were: 1.) Should it be a regional or federal government? 2.) Should it be a secular or religious government? and 3.) Who would get the oil money? Those are three big issues to resolve in a week, but they hobbled together a solution, and submitted it to parliament who reluctantly approved it and then it went to a public vote.

It passed with a small majority (remember the purple thumbs?) and became the law of the land, although nobody seemed happy with the solution and there has been constant wrangling over it ever since.

If you're in mediation and you narrow down the issues that way, there has to be a winner and there has to be a loser. Keep enough issues open so you can trade off one against another, and you can create a win-win solution where everyone feels that they've won.

Rule five: If you reach a deadlock, bring in a third party.

Here's my definition of a deadlock: Neither side sees any point in talking to each other.

If your personal problem has advanced to that stage, there is only one way to resolve it, and that is to bring in a third party as a mediator or an arbitrator.

There's a big difference between the two. A mediator doesn't have a lot of power. He or she is there to facilitate a solution. An arbitrator has a lot of power. With binding arbitration there will be a winner and there will be a loser. At the end of binding arbitration the arbitrator will decide who is at fault and what the penalty should be.

The key issue with both mediators and arbitrators is that they must be perceived as neutral by both sides. They cannot be effective unless they are perceived as neutral by both sides.

If you are dealing with a people problem it is unlikely that you'll choose arbitration. That's more applicable for money problems. You'll want to go with mediation.

You could hire a professional mediator, but a trusted psychotherapist would work also. Be sure that the person has mediation experience and knows how to mediate. Not all of them do.

There are many advantages to mediation. Here are the key ones:

➤ If you're not talking to the other person a mediator can get the parties to agree to another meeting. That's hard for the participants to do unless the other side is willing to change their position.

➤ They can be far more persuasive in dealing with the other person if they are perceived as neutral. You lose 80 percent of your ability to persuade people if they think you have something to gain from the attempt.

➧ Mediators can float trial balloons in an attempt to find acceptable solutions. The mediator can go to each side separately and suggest, "What if I could get them to agree to do this...?" If you were to approach the other side directly they may see it as a weakening of your position and a chance to increase their demands.

Rule six: Don't expect too much from the resolution to a problem.

If your people problem is that you haven't spoken to the other person for years be careful that you're not fantasizing about how great life will be once you're talking to each other again.

I once knew a woman who hadn't spoken to her son for 15 years and was torn apart by grief over the situation. She had no idea where her son was or what he had been doing since they last saw each other when he was 5 years old.

I went to extraordinary lengths to locate the son and get them together again, assuming that it would be the most wonderful thing that I could do for them. They stayed together for a year or two but then drifted apart again. The problems that had caused the rift were still there.

Your person problem may be tearing you apart but solving it is not going to solve all the problems in your life. Be realistic about what you can accomplish.

Having said that, if you've got someone in your life at whom you're hopping mad at, contacting him or her will be a very therapeutic thing for you to do.

I remember trying to persuade a young lady to do this. She had a father in Oregon whom she hadn't seen for many, many years. She held inside her an incredible amount of bitterness toward him, with very good reason. When she told me the things he'd done, I thought of the line in the song "How Can People Be So Heartless?" He was clearly a total jerk. I encouraged her to go to Oregon to meet him—not to forgive him or make friends with him but merely to make contact and complete the gap in this relationship, a gap that was affecting her enjoyment of the present moment so much.

She did, and when she returned she was positively glowing. Guess what she told me? Her father was still a jerk. However, now she could say it with a smile on her face. With this encounter, she had flushed away all the vitriolic feelings that had poisoned her system for years. She still didn't like him or choose to spend any time with him, and, to the best of my knowledge, she never saw him again. However, the meeting cleaned up her life.

If you have someone from whom you're estranged, you may be thinking just the opposite. Your thinking might be, "If I make contact with this person again, I'll feel responsible for them. They'll expect me to give them money and spend every weekend with them and I don't want to go there again." That's fine. You can create boundaries once you're talking to the person again. Even if you decide that you'll only have lunch together twice a year, you'll feel a lot better about yourself because you made contact.

Rule seven: Be sure that you're defining the problem properly.

Once a man e-mailed me from Italy, because he wanted to move to California. He felt he had a terrific business opportunity available to him and could be very successful. However, it would mean leaving behind his wife and his two young daughters, for at least five years.

A good problem-solver would know immediately he was making two very glaring errors. His first error? He wasn't defining the problem properly, which means laying out a clear picture of the entire problem or opportunity.

His second error? A very common one: He was jumping to the conclusion that he faced a dichotomy, meaning he thought

Solving People Problems

he only had the choice of moving to California, or not moving to California. A good problem solver would know that he had not categorized the problem properly.

I told him he'd be crazy to be away from his family for five years. He'd miss the chance of seeing his two young daughters grow up and mature into young women. His problem was, he'd reduced the situation to a dichotomy: either move to California and leave his family behind, or not move to California. What he should have been doing was using creative thinking to find a way he could move to California and still bring his family with him.

Rule eight: Analyze the consequence of potential solutions.

In another instance, a woman called me from San Francisco to tell me her husband had transferred to San Diego. He'd be there for at least a year and possibly longer than that. Then they'd promote him again and probably transfer him back to the head office in San Francisco Bay area. She couldn't decide whether to go through the trauma of selling their home, and moving to San Diego. Should she stay and wait for him to come back?

To a good problem-solver, this is a clear case of not thoroughly thinking through the consequences of what she was considering. A simple analysis would have given her a choice of consequences for each option that she was considering.

I advised her to get herself down to San Diego on the next plane, if she cared anything at all about her marriage. She wasn't thinking through the consequences of her actions. San Diego isn't Sioux City, Iowa. If she let her husband play bachelor in San Diego for a whole year, the chance of it destroying their marriage was high.

A simple reaction table would have told her that she had a great deal to lose and little to gain.

21

Rule nine: Don't confuse the issues.

In a third instance, a young man asked me a question at a seminar I conducted in Guangzhou, China. He wanted me to tell him if he should marry the woman he had been dating. He loved her, and she wanted to get married, but he wasn't so sure. Because of the Chinese "one child only" policy, men outnumber women in China. The Chinese Academy of Social Sciences in Beijing reports that there are now 120 males for every 100 females in China. You can imagine how hard that makes it for a man to find a bride.

In problem-solving terms, this is a clear case of not properly defining the problem, causing him to confuse two completely different issues.

Good problem solvers don't agonize over issues like this. They have a mental procedure they can follow very quickly, which to other people might seem instantaneous. In reality they're quickly going through a series of steps.

I'd never met the young lady, but I told him, yes, he should marry, but not marry that woman. His problem was he was tying together two separate decisions, and making them as if they were one decision. Yes, he should marry. I still think that it's the most wonderful thing any person can do (in spite of the fact that a survey by Pew Research and reported in a cover story in *Time* magazine showed that 40 percent of Americans think that marriage is obsolete). But if my young friend in China has to ask a complete stranger whether he should marry this woman or not, then the answer has to be no. When he finds the right person for him, he'll know it's the right decision and he won't be asking anyone, much less a complete stranger like me. I told him that when he finds the right woman wild horses won't stop him from marrying her—a bold response but one that caused a huge round of applause from my audience in Guangzhou.

➡ Key points from this chapter

▶ Don't try to sweep people problems under the rug. If the problem hasn't resolved itself in 48 hours you need to take action.

▶ Be careful that you're not overreacting to a situation. The last thing you need is to get a reputation of being so sensitive that people have to watch out for every word they say when they're around you.

▶ Establish and maintain communications at all cost. Unless you are able to talk to the person the situation is going to get worse.

▶ If you reach an impasse create momentum by reaching agreement on small issues.

▶ Don't narrow it down too far. Keep enough issues on the table to be able to trade off one for another so that both sides feel that they won.

▶ If you reach a deadlock bring in a third person as a mediator.

▶ The mediator cannot be effective unless perceived as neutral by both sides.

▶ Don't expect too much from resolution of the issue.

▶ Be sure that you're defining the problem well.

▶ Are you sure that you are considering all the possible solutions? Dichotomies are rare. Seldom do you have a problem where you only have two solutions from which to choose.

▶ Be sure to think through all the consequences of each solution.

▶ Be sure that you're defining the problem accurately. "Should I marry?" is not the same problem as "Should I marry this person?" "Should I go into business for myself?" is not the same as "Should I go into *this* business?"

> *Profit for a company is like oxygen for a person.*
> *If you don't have enough of it, you're out of the game.*
>
> —Peter Drucker

Chapter 3
Solving Money Problems

Now let's talk about money problems. Sufficient cash flow is essential to your success and well-being. Every businessperson learns, usually the hard way, that there is a big difference between assets and cash flow. You can have massive assets—large companies might have hundreds of millions in assets—and still go out of business because you lack cash flow. It's something about which businesses and families must be constantly diligent.

Don't feel ashamed that you lack the cash to pay your expenses. It can happen to the best of us. If General Motors can have a cash flow problem (and it has many times) you can, too.

Here's how to handle a shortage of cash in your business. The same rules apply to your personal finances.

You must make payroll

Your biggest business priority when you run out of cash is payroll. In business if you miss one payday, you are out of business. If you are not able to make a Friday payroll for your people, you will have to close the doors on Monday. If you can't make payroll on the 15th of the month, you must shut the doors on the 16th. Don't be fooled by thinking, "My people love me. They'll understand." No, they won't. Try missing one payday and see how much they love you.

Making payroll becomes your key priority. You need to do a cash flow projection for the next three months, using projected income figures that are realistic, not hopeful, and be sure that you will be able to meet payroll.

If it doesn't look as though you will have enough income to make payroll you're going to have to reduce your payroll costs. Nobody enjoys doing this, but it is essential to your survival.

As you think about the people who work for you, you will probably think of one or two people whom you wish would quit. Perhaps they've been with you a long time and you have a strong sense of loyalty to them. Perhaps they have been made redundant by technology. Are you still employing a full-time bookkeeper now that computers have made the job possible to do in one quarter of the time? Do you still have someone answering the phones when most of the calls go through to an answering system anyway? Do you still have a vice president of mimeographing locked away in the basement? If you've got anybody on payroll that you wish would make your life easier by quitting, you need to take action right away. Get them out of there!

If you're conflict averse it will probably occur to you that instead of firing people you should cut back everybody's hours. That may be a temporary solution if you are between orders and will need all of them in a month or two, but there's a real danger that you make everyone unhappy when you do that. It's better to let some people go and let them collect unemployment compensation for a while. Hopefully you'll be able to rehire them when business picks up. If you cut everyone's hours, you're just passing on your cash flow problem to your employees.

Here's a tip for you: Consider how conflict-averse you are. Some people love a good fight. Their idea of a fun evening is to go to bar and pick a fight with someone. If they are in the military, they want to be on the front lines where the action is. That's not me, and perhaps it's not you either. If you're conflict-averse, there's a high probability that you have failed to take the tough action that a businessperson in a cash flow crunch needs to have done.

Having terminated the people that you wish would have quit, consider the poor producers. Do you have salespeople that are having a tough time making their sales quota? Perhaps it's time to let them go and reassign your sales territories.

The key issue with reducing payroll costs is that you must be proactive. If you don't take control you'll find that the people who leave will be your best people because they have an easier time finding another job.

How to fire someone painlessly

I've fired dozens of people in my business career and I've never enjoyed doing it, but I did develop a way of doing it with as little pain as possible. Call them into your office and talk about the problems you're having until they realize that they're about to get fired. Then their interest is accepting your decision with the least amount of unpleasantness.

If the issue is their poor performance you might say, "Joe, when you joined us six months ago we had very high hopes for your performance. We set some challenging sales goals for you but felt confident that you would make them. As you're well aware, that hasn't happened. As of the end of last month you're still 28 percent off of your quota and that's just unacceptable." At this point Joe is getting the idea that he's going to get fired and wants to get out of there gracefully just as much as you do.

If the issue is a bad economy you might say, "I'm sure you're aware that we've been going through some very tough times lately. Business is down 38 percent from last year and we've come to the point when we have to adjust our payroll. We hate to let anyone go, of course, but it's come to the point where we have to take action or risk being out of business altogether."

Be sure that you have firmness and certainty in your voice. You are telling about a decision that you've made, not starting a conversation or, worse yet, an argument.

Get back to your core business

If you run a formerly successful business that is now suffering a cash flow problem, I'm pretty sure that I can identify your problem: *You have diversified away from your core business.*

A good friend of mine used to be a business consultant for a nationwide consulting firm. His job was to go into a company and investigate their business problems. He told me, "Roger, almost invariably I knew what their problem was the first day I got there. But I couldn't tell them then because I had to justify the huge bill that we were going to send them. I would work diligently for a couple of weeks and then tell them.

"If a company was big enough to pay us our fee it meant that they had at one time been very successful. Their problem was that they had diversified away from their core business. Perhaps they were eager to grow and had already saturated their industry. Sometimes they just got bored and wanted a new challenge. Sometimes they had developed a Messianic complex. They were convinced that they were so good that they couldn't fail at whatever they tried. My advice was always the same: Cut out the fringe stuff you're doing and get back to your core business."

Does that apply to your business? Have you expanded your product line or the services you offer to the point where the profit from your core business is just going to subsidize the money you're losing in your fringe businesses?

Control your expenditures

The next step is to get control of your expenditures. You must defer all capital expenditures—no new equipment, no unnecessary trips or purchases, unless they will result in income. You need to take personal control of this. Let all your people know that every expenditure over $20 must be approved by you in advance.

However, don't overreact. Don't frustrate your people by nickel and diming them to death. They need pens with which to write, they need paper to write on, and they need to be able to pick up the phone. You can contain your expenditures by controlling the larger items such as travel, long distance calls, and equipment purchases without making it difficult for your people to function from day to day.

Prioritize your bills

Next you need to go through all of your bills and prioritize them like this:

A. Must be paid now or you're out of business. This would include utilities, telephone, and Internet connections.

B. Are critical to be paid (such as rent). Contact these people and use your negotiating skills to get them to give you concessions. In a cash flow crisis you tend to think that some things (like lease payments) are non-negotiable. Don't think that way. Everything can be re-negotiated.

C. Do not need to be paid now (such as bills from vendors, printing, promotional supplies).

Contact the B and C bills when they are 30 days past the due date and explain that you are in a temporary cash flow problem because some key customers let you down. It's important that you contact them before they call you to complain about slow payment. If it's already too late for that, call anyway.

You must take a very firm stand on this issue. Resist the temptation to pay a vendor who is angry with you. Resist the temptation to pay off small bills, because you can afford to. It's essential that you get these payments deferred so that you can build up a reserve of operating cash. Do not agree to any late payment or interest charges. If vendors ask you for penalties, tell them forcefully that to do that would only put you further into trouble, and you cannot agree to that.

You are going to have to talk very strongly to some creditors. You may have to tell them, "You can take me to court if you want, but it's going to take you two years to get your case heard. Plus it would only force me to declare Chapter 13. Only 10 percent of firms that file bankruptcy ever recover, so then you'll never get paid. If you'll work with me you will get paid."

Some larger creditors may ask you to sign a personal guarantee for the loan if you want it extended. You should never do this.

Partners profit distributions

You cannot justify paying the partners profits when there are no profits to distribute. You should still receive your salary for running the company and expense reimbursement for company business, but you cannot pay yourself a profit distribution. You must defer this outflow of cash. And of course the same has to apply to any shareholders or venture capitalists.

Arrange a line of credit before you need it

If you have financial backers, approach them now, explain the problem, and (very important) outline in detail what you are doing to correct the problem. Tell them that you hope you don't need it, but you need to know that you could draw on a line of credit if necessary.

Approach your banker for a business line of credit. One that you will only draw upon if you need it. Do not sign a personal guarantee.

Set a personal example for your people

Your people need to see that you, too, are on the austerity program. Avoid taking clients to expensive restaurants. If you have a staff meeting, where you normally would have gone to a restaurant, have it in the office instead and order in sandwiches or pizza. If they see that you are being frugal, they will also hold down their expenses.

Remain cheerful, calm, and confident

As we say in sailing, "The crew must never see fear in the captain's eyes." You need to display leadership skills here. Don't confide in even your closest employees that you are worried. Let them know that you understand the problem and you know what to do. You are taking some tough corrective measures right now, but everything will work out fine.

Remember that worry never solved anything. Focus on the solution to the problem, not the problem.

Avoiding future cash flow problems

Having survived a cash flow problem, you need to take action to avoid a repeat of the problem in the future. Most people who survive a cash flow crisis are so "scared straight" that they'll do anything to avoid another one, but let's talk about how you're going to do that.

You must a have a written business and personal financial plan. It's not good enough to be thinking, "I've always been able to survive in the past. I can handle the problem if it comes up." Acknowledge that you may not be hard-wired for detailed planning. It may not be your strong suit. Perhaps you think of yourself as risk taker who is successful simply because you take financial risks when others wouldn't have the courage. Forget all that. You need a written and personal financial plan.

If that seems like the most boring thing in the world to you, you need to get somebody to do it for you. You need someone who can warn you when you're slipping into financial problems.

Life is a lot less stressful when you've got money in your pocket

This may sound ridiculously elementary, but you've got to start saving money for when you'll need it.

A young person called me for advice. She was overwhelmed by the stress of everyday living. I told her that things are a lot easier when you've got money. I can remember when I was young and I had to spend $20 to fix my car. Coming up with $20 was a problem when I was just getting started. It ruined my day. Life is a lot easier when you've got a Ben Franklin folded up in the corner of your wallet.

Start saving money now. When I first got a job and was making $93 a week, I would take $18.75 of that and buy a U.S. savings bond each week. It cost only $18.75 to purchase, but would be worth $25 when it matured. When you're grossing $93 a week it takes a great deal of discipline, extreme dedication, and a strong desire for a better life, to keep you from succumbing to the temptation to dip into your savings. Those meager savings enabled me to buy my first house the following year, and my second one the year after that.

Mike Summey, my writing partner on the Weekend Millionaire series of real estate investing books, got his fortune started by saving the change from his pockets. He had a big old plastic water bottle in his closet and filled it up with his loose change at the end of the day.

If this is too elementary for you, please pass it on to a young person who hasn't figured it out yet. If they would avoid running up credit card debt and have the discipline to delay purchases until they can pay cash, it will eventually make them millions of dollars.

The same advice applies if you own a big company. Put a little of your profits into a liquid investment fund so that you won't suffer a cash flow problem in the future.

➡ Key points from this chapter

▸ Having cash flow is more critical than having assets.

▸ A cash flow crisis can happen to the best and the largest of companies.

▶ You must make payroll. If you can't make payroll you're out of business, however loyal you think your employees are.

▶ Take the pain out of letting people go by talking about the situation until they realize they're getting fired.

▶ If you have diversified, get back to your core business.

▶ Control your expenditures. Let your people know that they can't spend more than $20 without your okay.

▶ Prioritize your bills. *A* bills must be paid or you're out of business. *B* bills are critical to be paid but perhaps you can renegotiate. *C* bills need to be paid eventually but not during the cash flow crisis.

▶ Suspend all payments to partners and investors.

▶ Arrange a line of credit before you need it. Approach your investors first and then your bankers. Don't let them talk you into a personal guarantee.

▶ Be frugal in all your activities so that your people can see that you feel their pain and are serious about controlling expenses.

▶ Never let your people see fear in your eyes.

▶ Have a written business and personal financial plan. It that's too boring for you, find someone who loves detail work and have him or her do it for you.

▶ Start saving money now so you won't have another cash flow problem.

Section Two

Problem~Solving Tools

The release of atomic energy has not created a new problem. It has merely made more urgent the necessity of solving an existing one.

—Albert Einstein

In this section I'm going to teach you some fundamentals about solving problems. You'll learn how a 14th-century Franciscan monk living in a small village in England created a problem-solving rule that is still used today. You may remember it being a major part of the plot of the movie *Contact*. If you're a fan of the television medical drama *House*, you'll recall that it was a big part of the plot in an early episode.

You'll find out what Sakichi Toyoda, the founder of Toyota Corp. preached when faced with a problem. It applies to just about any problem from the "my car won't start" variety to the most major corporate problems.

Very often problems cause angry behavior, so I'll tell you how to deal with that in Chapter 6. If you've ever lost your temper and regretted it, you will benefit from learning what Roman Emperor Nero's tutor had to say about it.

You'll learn why many problems are already solved because the solution is in your mission statement, and how some problems don't deserve your attention because you can solve them using parameters.

I'll teach why you should always verify details before you seek a solution.

When faced with a "do we or don't we" type of problem the one question you should always ask yourself is, "What happens if I do nothing?" We'll talk about that in Chapter 10.

To finish up the section we'll talk about when and how you should get help with your problem.

Chapter 4

The Simplest Solution Is the Most Likely

In the movie *Contact* Jodie Foster and Matthew McConaughey are at a Washington cocktail party debating the possible existence of God. Jodie is not a believer. She is a scientist who wants empirical evidence before she'll believe anything. He is an intensely religious believer who feels that faith, by sheer definition, is belief in God without empirical proof.

Jodie Foster: "It's like you're saying that science kills God. What if science reveals that He never existed in the first place?" Matthew McConaughey escorts her out to the patio. Jodie says, "I've got one for you. Have you ever heard of Occam's Razor? It's a scientific principle. It says that, all things being equal, the simplest solution tends to be the right one. Which is more likely? That an all powerful guy created the universe and decided not to give any proof of his existence, OR He simply doesn't exist at all and we created Him so that we wouldn't have to feel so small and alone?

Matthew McConaughey: "I couldn't imagine a world where God didn't exist. I wouldn't want to."

Jodie Foster: "How do you know you're not deluding yourself. For me, I'd need proof."

What's Occam's Razor all about? Occam is a tiny village in Surrey County, England, about 15 miles from where

I was born and not far from the M25 ring freeway that circles London. (These days it's spelled Ockham.) It probably would have faded into intellectual oblivion centuries ago if it weren't for a fellow named John who lived in Occam and fancied himself a bit of a philosopher. This was in the 14th century, so long ago that people didn't even have surnames. John was known as John of Occam. He first postulated the theory to which Jodie Foster refers: Occam's Razor. Strangely enough he never actually stated what we now call the scientific principle named after him that says all things being equal, the simplest solution tends to be the right one.

What he did say (in Latin, which was the language of 14th-century English intellectuals) were two principles:

1. **The Principle of Plurality.** *Plurality should not be posited without necessity.* In simpler language that means don't make it more complicated than it has to be.

2. **The Principle of Parsimony:** *It is pointless to do with more what is done with less.* If you can solve a problem with a simple solution, what's the point of looking for a more complicated solution?

It was future generations of philosophers who promoted the theory of simplicity in his name, no doubt buttressed by the knowledge that John was a Franciscan monk who took his vow of poverty seriously. He did live a very simple life.

Occam's Razor (the razor part refers to the process of shaving down more complicated explanations to get at the truth) is not a problem-solving tool. It doesn't prove anything. It's a heuristic devise, a way of suggesting solutions.

Let's say that someone presents you with a light bulb that turns on without being screwed in. It looks like a regular light bulb but it lights up without being attached to anything. How could that be? Think about it for a while and you might come up with three possible solutions:

1. They have invented a way of transporting electricity through the air like a radio wave.

2. They have found a way to conceal the electrical cord so that I can't see it.

3. They have hidden a battery inside the stem of the bulb.

I've listed those three explanations from the most complicated to the simplest. Occam's Razor suggests to you that number three is the simplest and therefore the most likely answer.

Let's look at a more complicated problem: the sudden appearance of crop circles in farmers' wheat fields. In 1991 circles started appearing in fields near Southampton, England. It didn't attract much attention. Soon another, more complicated pattern appeared in Matterly Bowl, a natural phenomenon that is visible from several main roads. This raised a lot of publicity, and public opinion on the cause of the phenomenon went wild. Suddenly crop circles were popping up all over the place. The designs became more and more complicated.

Conspiracy theorists had a field day and had half of England convinced that extra-terrestrials from outer space were landing at night to send us messages. A simple application of Occam's Razor would have solved the problem. The thought that extra-terrestrials were responsible was the most complicated solution. The simplest solution was that humans were doing it as a prank.

Meanwhile, Doug Bower (the secret perpetrator of the circles) had a marital problem. His wife thought he was having an affair because he would frequently disappear overnight. She tracked the mileage on his car to determine that he was driving long distances. (In England, 50 miles is considered a long journey. You can never be more than 72 from the sea, which would be the distance from Coton in the Elms, Derbyshire, to the North Sea, according to the government ordinance survey.) Evidently fearing his wife more than the wrath of the farmers whose fields he was damaging, he confessed that he and a friend of his had caused the circles.

If you're a fan of the television series *House* you'll remember that the third episode of the first season was named "Occam's Razor." House's students at his infectious diseases ward in a New Jersey hospital are convinced that their patient has a previously unknown exotic disease. House argues that the answer is simpler—that somebody screwed up his treatment.

Why does Occam's Razor work? Why is the simplest solution the most likely? Good question. I don't know why. It's why apples fall off trees and hit philosophers, I suppose. It's just one of the laws of our universe. Remember that John of Occam was living in a very simple world. He was not concerned with tsunamis in Japan or trapped miners in Chile.

We live in the very complicated world that is hard for us to comprehend. That alone makes Occam's Razor a more valuable tool than it was in John's day. Remember that, when your IT expert is going through reams of paperwork that explain why horse food sales are down. Maybe it's just because the horses don't like the way it tastes. If you're still saying, "Yes, but I need to understand why Occam's Razor works," I suggest that you reread Occam's Razor.

While strangely named Occam's Razor may not be a problem-solving tool it will serve you as a very useful heuristic or problem-solving device. When faced with trying to understand a problem, consider the simplest solutions to be the most likely.

➠ Key points from this chapter

▶ Occam's Razor suggests the simplest answer is the most likely.

▶ It is not a problem-solving tool because it doesn't prove anything, but it is very helpful when trying to determine the answer to a problem.

▶ List possible solutions from the most complicated to the simplest. The most likely explanation will be the simplest.

Chapter 5
The Five Whys of Problem Solving

Sakichi Toyoda was a pretty smart fellow by anybody's standards. Born in 1867 in Japan, where his father was a poor carpenter, he created one of the greatest industrial companies this planet has ever known. The Japanese came to call him the king of Japanese inventors and the father of that country's industrial revolution. He invented the Toyoda loom, sold it to an English mill for one million yen, and used the money to start the eponymously named Toyota Company.

Sakichi is famous in problem-solving circles for the developing the concept of the *five whys*: that when you have a problem you should ask *why* five times to find the source of the problem and prevent the problems from recurring.

Let's start out with a simple automobile problem:

1. Problem: My car won't start. *Why?*

2. Answer: The battery is dead. *Why?*

3. Answer: The alternator was not charging the battery when I last drove it. *Why?*

4. Answer: The alternator belt was broken. *Why?*

5. Answer: Because I failed to maintain the car. *Why?*

Answer: I was not committed to following the scheduled car maintenance program. *What must I do to prevent reoccurrence?* Commit to regularly inspecting and maintaining the vehicle.

The *five whys* formula discourages you from quitting when you find the first solution. Realizing that the battery was dead may have caused you to recharge or replace the battery. But the problem would recur if you didn't persist with a solution. Replacing the alternator wouldn't solve the problem unless you determine that the belt was broken. You must determine the cause of the problem, not just treat the symptoms.

Note that the *five whys* is not an absolute number. In this case a sixth why would have been helpful: Why did the belt break? Is it rubbing against something? Or you could reasonably stop at three whys and replace the alternator belt and hope that the alternator was not also faulty.

But Sakichi Toyoda intended the *five whys* to take you to the point where you determined what you would have to do to stop the problem from recurring.

Let's take a look at a more complicated problem, which is a well-known exercise in problem-solving circles. Here's how Outward Bound describes it in their training manual:

Problem: The National Park Service has determined that the Washington Monument is deteriorating.

1. *Why* is the monument deteriorating?
    Because the park service uses harsh chemicals to clean the monument.

2. *Why* are harsh chemicals used?
    The harsh chemicals are needed to clean the bird droppings. There are a lot of birds.

3. *Why* are there a lot of birds?
    Because the birds eat the spiders. There are a lot of spiders.

4. *Why* are there a lot of spiders?
   Because the spiders eat the gnats. There are a lot of gnats.

5. *Why* are there a lot of gnats?
   Because the lights at dusk attract the gnats.

Solution: Turn the lights on 30 minutes later.

The benefits of the five whys method.

It's simple and easy to teach.

It focuses on root causes and forces participants to go beyond obvious failings of the equipment or method being investigated.

It's flexible, so it works well with other problem solving and root cause detection methods.

➠ Key points from this chapter

▸ Asking the *five whys* is a great way to determine the root cause of a problem.

▸ Persist through the *five whys* and don't be tempted to quit when you find a problem. It may not be the only problem.

▸ Don't let its simplicity fool you. It's a key technique that is used worldwide to solve problems by determining the root cause.

Chapter 6

Don't Let Anger Exacerbate Your Problem

In my negotiating training I teach that it's okay to get upset with people when you're negotiating, as long as you're in control and doing it as a specific negotiating tactic. It's when you get upset and lose control that you get into trouble.

How angry do you get? Is your lack of anger control creating problems for you? If you've ever thrown a chair across a basketball court, ripped a phone off the wall, or tossed a golf club into a lake, you need what we're going to talk about in this chapter. If this doesn't apply to you but you know someone who needs it and are afraid to tell him or her about his or her problem, you have my permission to photo copy this chapter and leave it on his or her desk anonymously!

The first thought that may occur to you is that sometimes your anger is good for you. It convinces your toddler to run away from an advancing car. It stops your dog from digging under your fence and disappearing. It forcefully commands a child or an employee to obey you.

Philosophers have debated this for a couple of thousand years now, so you're just in time to contribute your two cents. Aristotle would agree that you need anger sometimes. Seneca would vigorously disagree. Seneca was a very interesting fellow who became one of the richest and most influential people in ancient Rome. Seneca was born in Spain to a very wealthy family. His father made frequent trips to Rome with the intention of becoming an advocate, an occupation that roughly translates to high court lawyer. The son went with him and studied rhetoric (the art of using language to communicate and persuade) and philosophy, and become an accomplished orator at a very young age. He had the great misfortune to be appointed tutor to the future Emperor Nero, who turned out to be murderous psychopath who wouldn't let Seneca quit, however hard he tried.

Inevitably he ran afoul of Nero's temper, who accused him unfairly of plotting against him. The charges were probably trumped up but Seneca had become a very wealthy and powerful man by then, and that alone would have incurred Nero's wrath sooner or later. Seneca became famous for two things: a book that he wrote titled *On Anger,* and the way in which he died.

In his book he argued that anger was never useful. (You can Google the entire book because the copyright has expired long ago.) How did he die? Nero sent a centurion to accuse Seneca of treason and demand that he immediately kill himself. Seneca responded by pulling out a knife and slashing his veins. Although much admired by Romans as a noble act, it would have been forgotten if, some 1,700 years later, Belgian painter Peter Rubens and French painter Jacques Louis David had not created amazing paintings of Seneca dying in this bathtub surrounded by his grief-stricken friends and family.

In his brilliant book *The Consolations of Philosophy* British philosopher Alain de Botton argues that we can learn a lot from the way that Seneca died. The key to controlling your anger, he insists, is to lower your expectations of other people. Anger comes from having unrealistic expectations about the way life and other people will treat you.

What angers you? Is it your morning commute and all the selfish, uncaring, and unskilled drivers out there? But wait a minute. Aren't they always out there? Shouldn't you have adjusted to this fact now? For one week try adjusting your attitude to this situation. Think to yourself every morning, "I'm going out to the freeway today to be with every selfish, uncaring, and unskilled driver in the state. I accept this as the way things are, and I refuse to let it upset me." If you lower your expectations of other people you will be able to control your anger.

I thought that I'd test Alain's theory when a yacht club friend of mine came to me with a problem. He loved to go sailing with his 25-year-old son but every time they went they ended up arguing with each other. The problem was that the father thought that he was doing most of the work while the son was having all the fun.

The father had to haul the mainsail up, prepare the jib sail for unfurling, stow the fenders, and take off and store the main sail cover. Upon their return the father would have to hop off the boat to tie it down at the slip, stow the main sail, and install the sail and winch covers. Meanwhile the son had all the pleasure of sitting in the cockpit, drinking beer, and steering the boat.

I told the father about Seneca's advice on anger and suggest that in future he go sailing with his son without any expectation that the son would do any of the work.

It made an almost-miraculous change in their relationship. The father no longer got upset over his son not doing any work and started appreciating whatever little thing he did do. Because his father was no longer nagging him to do more, the son started to do more of the work.

I'm sure you're thinking, "Wait a minute. That's no way to raise a son. He'll always be lazy." That may be so, but if you just focus on the father's anger, it's a very effective way of solving the problem.

Do you side with Seneca, who wrote that anger is never a good thing? Or with Aristotle, who wrote, "Anybody can become angry, that is easy; but to be angry with the right person, and to the right degree, and at the right time, and for the right purpose, and in the right way, that is not within everybody's power, that is not easy"?

I think that what I teach at my negotiating seminars is the answer. It's okay to get upset with people, as long as you're in control and doing it as a specific tactic. It's when you get upset and lose control that you get into trouble.

If you find yourself creating problems by losing your temper, take Alain de Botton's advice and lower your expectations of what fate has in store for you and how other people treat you.

➥ Key points from this chapter

▶ It's okay to get upset with people, as long as you're in control and doing it as a specific tactic. It's when you get upset and lose control that you get into trouble.

▶ Is anger sometimes good for you? Doesn't it help solve problems? Philosophers have disagreed on this.

▶ Greek philosopher Aristotle advises learning to use anger "with the right person, and to the right degree, and at the right time, and for the right purpose, and in the right way."

▶ Roman philosopher Seneca felt that anger was never good for you.

▶ British modern-day philosopher Alain de Botton believes that losing your temper is caused by having too high expectations for what happens to you and the way people treat you.

▶ Lower your expectations and you will not lose your temper.

Chapter 7
Let Your Principles
Guide You

A key question to ask yourself is: Is the problem covered by an existing policy or personal principle? That's one of the first and key things to look for. Is there an existing policy or personal principle that tells you whether you should go ahead or not?

> "I run a company in Seattle that distributes garden tools and equipment. One of my buyers told me about a container of ten speed bikes that's on the water, only five days out from port. The chain of stores that had ordered them declared bankruptcy, and I can pick them up for 25 cents on the dollar. My problem is that it sounds like easy money, but I can't decide."

This is a problem best answered by referring to policy. You're in the gardening equipment business. Your corporate mission statement probably tells you that you shouldn't get into the bicycle business. However much money you could make, you shouldn't be tempted.

Roy Disney used to say that decision-making is easy when values are clear. I'm not just talking about corporate policy here. Individuals should have clear principles. It makes problem solving easier. If something comes up that violates your principles, your ethics, or your morals, you won't do it regardless of the temptation.

One of the reasons that Nordstrom Department Stores is so successful is their policy manual. The entire thing is one page long.

Nordstrom's Policy Manual

"Welcome to Nordstrom. We're glad to have you with our company. Our number one goal is to provide outstanding customer service. Set both your personal and professional goals high. We have great confidence in your ability to achieve them. Nordstrom's rules: Rule 1: Use your good judgment in all situations. There will be no additional rules."

One of the most successful grocery stores in the country, Stew Leonard's in Connecticut, has its policy manual engraved in a rock outside its front door. It's two paragraphs long:

Stew Leonard's Policy Manual

Rule 1. The customer is always right.

Rule 2. If the customer is ever wrong, reread rule one.

Isn't that a great policy? If you want to go into a business where the customer is always wrong, become a policeman, not a store owner.

Imagine how many times a day employees at Nordstroms or Stew Leonard's wonders whether they should or shouldn't do something. Then they think of the company policy, and know what to do.

When I was young, I was the merchandise manager at the Montgomery Ward store in Bakersfield, California. Although Bakersfield was a small agricultural community, we ranked in the top 15 stores out of 600 nationwide. We did it with a determination to keep our customers happy at all cost. I would tell the department managers, "If you have a customer who wants you to give them a refund or an adjustment, give it to them. Because if you send them up to my office I will give it to them, so you might as well be the hero."

Back to the Seattle garden tool-distributing company. Perhaps its company mission statement is broad enough to permit the president to buy the container of ten-speed bikes. Perhaps it says "We will become the most profitable distributor of garden equipment in the Northwest, by offering the finest service at competitive prices. Also we will take advantage of opportunities to make money in other areas." That's fine, because I'm not telling him how to run his business, but I am saying he'll be more successful if he has a clear mission statement that everybody who works there understands.

Individuals' policies are called principles

It's important that you have a personal policy to guide you also. A personal policy is what we call a principle. If we all are clear on our principles, a life plan against which we applied our problem solving and decision-making, we could free up vast stores of energy for the really important things.

Let's take the simple act of driving the car to the store. It's only a mile away—should we bother to put on the seat belt? If our personal policy/principle says that we always drive with a seat belt, there's no wasted energy making a decision. We slip it on almost without realizing it.

On the way to the store, the traffic signal turns yellow. A surge of adrenaline occurs. Should we go for it, or hit the brakes? If our personal policy/principle is that we always stop for yellow lights, we stop calmly, without wasted energy.

A car is standing in a driveway, waiting for an opening to pull into traffic. Should we wave it ahead of us, or let it wait? With our principles clear, there's no hesitation.

Now please understand that I'm not telling you how to drive, although I do care about your safety. If your personal policy tells you to gun it for yellow lights, or never wear a seat belt, and never let a jerk pull in front of you, that—I suppose—is your business. The point I'm making here is that if you don't have a personal policy by which you run your days, you're operating an inefficient, energy-wasting life.

If you waste that much nervous energy just driving to the store, imagine how much waste there is in an *organization* that doesn't have a clear company policy! I've been in organizations like that. The leader has everybody on such a tight rein that people at all levels agonize over decisions, wondering whether the boss will agree with what they're about to do. Because the game plan changes every week, people can never be sure that what was the right way to solve a problem last week will still be the way to go this week. The organizations that do have a clear policy are a joy with which to work. As Roy Disney said, when values are clear, decision-making is easy.

Is your problem covered by your policies?

The third question is to see if it fits your corporate and personal policies. If it does, you either follow policy, or consider changing the policy. You don't make random exceptions to the policy.

If you don't already have a policy for this problem, you should then consider if it's likely to recur. If it's likely to recur, you should establish a policy that tells you how to handle it the next time it comes up.

When I say policy, I'm not just talking about your corporate policy and procedures manual. It applies to your personal life, too. If your son disobeys your instructions, and comes home late, do you ground him, or don't you? Think it through, and establish a policy. Not only will you get more respect from your children because you're consistent, but also you'll save a lot of nervous energy. Because the next time it happens, you won't have to waste time agonizing over how to solve the problem. That doesn't mean you become an inflexible tyrant. Your children should always know they could appeal to you for an exception to policy if they have a good enough reason.

After you've made a decision, it's important to decide if you need a policy to handle this if it comes up again. Whenever you solve a problem, think to yourself, "Is it likely to recur?" If you set up a policy, all future responses can be programmed. When the problem recurs, it doesn't require another decision.

People unconsciously do this all the time. A 4-year-old uses a swear word in front of his father. The father whops him upside the head. The boy creates policy to handle this in the future. Usually it's "Don't swear in front of Dad anymore."

You probably know somebody who lost everything during the Great Depression. They then made a policy of never borrowing money on real estate again. They didn't know they'd created a policy, and it wasn't smart, but it stayed with them for the rest of their lives.

Problem solving shapes your life; you become the sum total of all the problems you solve. But what's even more important is whether you make a policy, after you solve a problem. If the problem is likely to come up again, write a policy to handle it in the future. That's what really shapes the rest of your life. And that's what really shapes the future of your company.

➡ Key points from this chapter

- ▸ Is it covered by an existing policy? If not, should a policy be created to handle this when it comes up again?

- ▸ If it doesn't conform to your policy, you can still decide to do it, but you have to change your policy to adapt to it.

- ▸ Don't make random exceptions to your policy.

- ▸ Develop a personal policy by which you run your life. We call that your principles. It removes a great deal of stress from your life and saves your energy for more important things.

Chapter 8
Does the Problem
Deserve a Decision?

This is a short chapter but it makes a key point: that we all waste a lot of time trying to make a decision on something that doesn't deserve a decision.

> "I was driving from Dallas to Houston. I'd planned to spend the night in Houston, out by the International Airport, but with 90 miles still to go, I found myself dozing at the wheel. I started looking for a place to spend the night. I saw a billboard for a motel, but as I was about to pull off, I saw another billboard that looked better, so I kept going. Several times I was tempted to pull off, but I kept on going in the hope of finding something better. I just didn't seem able to decide."

Because the long-term consequences aren't great, this is a problem that should immediately be solved by establishing parameters.

The person in the story should decide what he won't accept, and take the first thing that doesn't violate the parameters. For example, he may say, "I'm not going to pay more than $75 for a room, it has to have a private bathroom, and it has to be clean." This means that the perfect decision here is to pull off the highway and take the first motel that meets those criteria.

Another example:

"I was on the late night flight home from a business trip. In the airport bookstore, I was looking for a book to read, in case I couldn't sleep on the plane. The more I looked, the harder the choice got."

Hey, come on! This situation doesn't justify a problem-solving technique. She should establish parameters, pick something, and move on. Perhaps she didn't want to pay for hardcover, didn't like romances or war stories, and she's too tired to read a business book. Anything else is okay, so she should pick the first book that falls within her parameters, and move on.

Always consider whether the problem even deserves your concern. How great are the long-term consequences? If consequences are not *that* great, use parameters to decide how you're going to solve the problem.

▶ Key points from this chapter

▶ Does your problem deserve a decision?

▶ If not, establish parameters, and pick the first choice that falls within them.

Chapter 9
Is the Problem Real or
Imagined?

Before you start finding the solution to your problem, you must decide whether the problem or opportunity is real or imagined. All too often we overreact and spend time and energy on problems and opportunities that are illusions. In many newsrooms, you'll find a big sign that says: "Nothing is as bad or as good as it's first reported." It teaches the reporters not to overreact.

Doesn't that happen in corporations? There's a rumor that a key person is quitting, and suddenly everyone's mind is running through all the different possibilities and decisions that need to be made. What you need to be doing first is confirming or denying the rumor, instead of automatically jumping into a problem-solving process.

The same thing applies to opportunities. Is it a real opportunity or only an apparent opportunity?

Somebody calls to tell us a company in our industry is for sale. We tend to go immediately into a mental decision-making mode: Could we handle the acquisition? How would our employees react? What if a competitor bought it and pumped millions of dollars into it?

What we should be doing first is finding out if it really is for sale. If so, how much are they asking for it, and can it be bought on a leveraged buy-out or in exchange for stock? At this point, you're seeing if you can locate a disqualifier: You continue to gather information unless you run across something that rules out the acquisition. It's smart to gather this information well ahead of making a decision. You're really investigating to see if a decision needs to be made—to see if it's a real opportunity or just an apparent opportunity. If it's only imagined, quit worrying. Relax and back off, because unless you overreact, nothing's going to happen.

Be sure that you understand it properly. I was playing golf at my club once when one of the other players said, "Is anybody thinking of buying a new driver? I've got a new one so I'm giving this away." The thought that he might give me his driver got me excited. Then I found out that his interpretation of "giving it away" really meant exchanging it for $200 of my money. I still bought the driver and was happy with it but it taught me a simple but important lesson: Verify an opportunity or a problem before you pursue it.

➤ Key points from this chapter

- ▶ Before you spend energy deciding what to do about a problem or an opportunity, verify that it is real.

- ▶ Be sure that you fully understand the situation.

Chapter 10

What Happens If You Do Nothing?

Next you need to ask yourself what happens if you decide to do *nothing*? Will the situation improve or deteriorate?

Since the publication of my book *Secrets of Power Negotiation*, many readers call my office if they're involved in a negotiation and need help. I'm always happy to help them if I'm there. If I'm away on a speaking trip, I'll always return the call when I get back into town. Through the years, I've learned an interesting thing: If I'm out of town and not able to call them back for a few days, in over half the cases, the problem has gone away by the time I reach them. In more than half the cases, the best solution to the problem was to make no decision at all.

I told you earlier that there are only two types of problems, people problems and money problems. But within those categories, there are many different kinds of problems. For example:

▶ You have many choices but you don't know which one to pick.

▶ You don't see any solution to the problem.

▶ It's a *do we or don't we* decision: Do we buy the new office building or don't we? Do we hire this person or don't we?

Any time you are faced with a *do we or don't we* decision you first thought should be "What happens if we do nothing"?

The decision to invade the Branch Davidian compound in Waco, Texas, was a *do we or don't we* decision. A religious sect had barricaded itself into the Mount Carmel religious retreat. When ATF officers approached their compound to determine if they were breaking gun laws, four of them were shot and killed.

Hundreds of law-enforcement officers laid siege to the compound. The incident became a national affair, and it fell to Attorney General Janet Reno to decide what to do. After a 51-day standoff she gave orders to invade. The defenders promptly set fire to the compound and 76 died in an horrific mass suicide.

Janet Reno should have thought, "What happens if we do nothing?" She explained that she had to act because children were being abused inside the compound. Sorry, Janet, but this was simply untrue. When the FBI sent food supplies in to the rebels they cleverly planted microphones in the milk cartons. They could hear every word spoken, and you can read the transcripts on the Internet. There was no child abuse.

It should have been clear to the authorities that there was no compelling reason to invade. The right solution to the problem would have been to cordon off the area and do nothing. By the time the FBI was faced with the Montana Freemen rebellion three years later they had learned the lesson. They did nothing, and 81 days later the rebels surrendered without a shot being fired.

Before you take action determine this: If you do nothing, will the problem get worse, or better? If it isn't going to get worse, give it some time and see if it doesn't go away.

➥ Key points from this chapter

▶ When you are faced with a go or no go decision you should first consider "What happens if we do nothing?"

▶ If nothing bad will happen you should wait it out.

▶ When there are no negative consequences half of your problems will go away if you give them time.

To solve any problem, here are three questions to ask yourself:
First, what could I do?
Second, what could I read?
And third, who could I ask?

—Jim Rohn

Chapter 11

Is the Problem Really Unique?

Before you start fretting that your life is going to be ruined by the problem you face, ask yourself this: Is the problem really unique?

Once you've decided that, everything else is automatic. You'll know how you can solve the problem from that point on.

If you're bogged down with solving a problem, it's probably because *you* haven't faced it before. Assuming that's true, there are three possibilities:

1.   Somebody else has faced the same problem.
2.   Nobody has faced this decision before.
3.   Underlying causes are exacerbating the problem.

Somebody has faced this problem before

The first possibility is that although you haven't faced the problem before, somebody else has. This might be a situation where you have a sick relative, you're having family problems, or either personal or corporate financial problems. Where the problem is new to you, but not to other people, the solution is to consult an expert such as a doctor, attorney, or marriage counselor.

Sometimes you agonize for years over a problem you think is unique. Perhaps it's a child or sibling who develops a distressing mental disease. You agonize for years over what to do about the problem. It seems that you're the only person who has faced this dilemma before. Once you accept it's not unique—it's just new to you—you're astounded to find out there are experts out there who face the same problem dozens of times a week. A simple Google search will open up a mine of information.

First decide if other people have faced the problem. If they have, consult an expert.

Nobody has faced this decision before

The second possibility is that the problem is so unique that almost no one has faced this decision before. For example, Colleen McCullough—a neuroscientist turned writer and famous author of *The Thornbirds*—decided she wanted to move to remote Norfolk Island, a thousand miles north of Auckland, New Zealand, and write historical novels. Nobody has ever done this before. There's no one she can e-mail and say, "How did that work out for you?" This kind of decision requires a combination of creative thinking and analysis.

Underlying causes are exacerbating the problem

The third possibility, when the problem is new to you, is that of underlying causes exacerbating the problem. For example:

> "I own three greeting card stores and one of them is always losing money. Should I close it down?"

Because you have underlying problems involved that may be causing the problems, you need to first figure out those underlying problems. Then find an answer for those.

➡ Key points from this chapter

▶ Determine the uniqueness factor. Is it only new to you?

▶ Who has faced this before?

▶ Are there underlying factors affecting the problem, and do they need to be resolved first?

Section Three

Questions to Ask Before You Solve a Problem

A problem well stated is a problem half-solved.

—Charles Kettering

Assertive businesspeople often make the mistake of making snap judgments when they're faced with a problem. I suppose that their thinking is "I'm paid to know the answers to these problems."

You will come up with much better solutions if you slow down and consider all the aspects of the problem before you attempt a solution.

In this section we'll talk about difficulties defining the problem. This is a critical issue. If you've defined the problem properly, you're more than halfway to finding a perfect solution.

How fast you pick a solution is critical. It's important not to choose too quickly, but it's also important not to move too slowly. We'll tell you how to analyze your problem to decide how urgent it is.

It's important to decide on how to solve the problem and then give all your efforts to support that course of action. But it's also important to realize when you've made a mistake. If the horse drops dead, get off fast, as they say in rodeo.

In Chapter 17 we'll talk about how some of the most attractive solutions are completely unworkable.

Chapter 12
Difficulty Defining the Problem

You're now ready to define the problem. There are four problems that can now come up in accurately defining the problem:

1. Being too far from the problem.
2. Being too familiar with the problem.
3. Being too close to the problem.
4. Misstating the problem.

Being too far from the problem

First, you're too far from the problem to see it clearly. India's leaders saw the solution to all their economic problems as the need to industrialize the nation. Gandhi was much closer to the people in the countryside. He correctly saw the solution as teaching his people to be self sufficient in food production.

Barack Obama was frequently accused of spending too much time taking care of international problems, and not being close enough to the economic problems at home.

One of the most remarkably successful businesspeople of the 20th century, Armand Hammer of Occidental Petroleum, credited much of his success to his willingness to travel. His corporate jet was always standing by, ready to take him to face-to-face meetings anywhere in the world.

Being too far from the problem is at the heart of most employee problems. The grunt on the front line complains that the generals at HQ don't understand what they're up against: "Why don't they come down here, and see for themselves?" The assembly worker complains, "Management doesn't know what it's like down here."

Be sure you're close enough to the problem to know what's really going on. Don't wait until the peasants are storming the palace gates to find out that they aren't thrilled with the way you're running your empire!

Being too familiar with the problem

The second problem is you're too familiar with the problem. Try this exercise. Without looking at your watch, can you describe the face? Does it have numbers or strokes or diamonds? Does it have a second hand? Most of us can't say. We look at our watch a dozen times a day, but never actually see it.

That's why someone can be married to an alcoholic for years, and not realize that his or her spouse was sick. When friends finally confront him with the problem, he's amazed to find out that he was the last to know. He was simply too familiar with the problem, to be able to see it in perspective.

Frequently a mother of a special needs child has to be told by an outsider that something is wrong, because the mother is simply too familiar with the child to see the problem.

Business leaders tend to make broad assumptions about the way things are done in their industry. When I became president of a large real estate company, I was relatively new to the industry. Everybody told me to expect a 20 percent fall-out ratio, which means that only 80 percent of the contracts signed will ever close. You lose 20 percent because the buyers can't get the financing, or they have a falling out with the seller, or a problem with title or zoning. To our company, this would mean that more than $100 million in sales was falling through the cracks each year. To an outsider like me, it seemed obvious that the easiest sale to make would be the one we would otherwise lose. What could we do to reduce fallouts? "You're wasting your time, Roger," I was told. "That's just the way it is in our industry." In fact, there was a lot we could do. By teaching negotiating skills to our people, I was able to dramatically reduce the amount of lost business.

Being too close to the problem

The third problem is you're too close to the problem. See if you can solve this problem.

> Draw a straight line that goes through
> New York, Dallas, and San Francisco.

It's a difficult problem to solve because you're so close it. In your mind you automatically see a map of the United States. You see New York in the East, and then you see Dallas down South, and San Francisco over in the West. You automatically say, "You can't draw a straight line that goes through those three." Yet, I can add another condition to that problem, and you probably can solve it immediately. Let me rephrase the question: I want you to draw a straight line that goes through these three cities in this order. First New York, then San Francisco and then Dallas. That makes it easy doesn't it? You realize all you have to do is draw a line around the globe.

Another example of being too close to the problem was the development of BART, the subway system in the San Francisco Bay Area. The planners set out to solve the Bay Area's traffic problems. However, they got so absorbed with building a technologically brilliant system that they lost sight of the objective. The result is a technologically perfect system, touted as the quietist transit system in the country, that too few people want to ride.

We're about to repeat the problem in the central valley of California, where we're going to spend $3.5 billion building a high-speed train from Bakersfield to Fresno, 100 miles north. I lived in Bakersfield for three and a half miserable years. I understand the need to get out of there fast to escape the 110 degrees at midnight heat in the summer and the stranglehold tule fog in the winter, but nobody is going to want to ride a high-speed train to Fresno, because they would prefer to get into their pickup truck and tune the radio to Buck Owens.

What the planners need to do is solve the transportation of the public, not create an engineering masterpiece.

Misstating the problem

The fourth problem with defining is misstating the problem. *Should I marry this person?* is different from *Should I marry?* And again, it's completely different from *Should I live with and have children with this person?*

We went to war with Iraq because we thought the problem was assuring a continuous supply of Middle East oil. That was attacking the symptoms of the problem instead of attacking the problem itself. The problem is our dependency on foreign oil.

In the preceding chapters, I've taught you how to define the problem accurately so you can get a clear picture of the decision you're facing. Good problem solvers agree with James Thurber that it's much better to know some of the right questions, than to think you know all of the right answers.

▪ Key points from this chapter

There are four difficulties with accurately defining the problem:

- ▶ Being too far from the problem.
- ▶ Being too familiar with the problem.
- ▶ Being too close to the problem.
- ▶ Misstating the problem.

Chapter 13
Don't Solve Problems Too Quickly

Acting too quickly probably causes more bad choices than anything else. There are three rules to follow, if you want to avoid this trap:

1. Beware of solving problems too quickly because of time pressure.
2. Don't make choices quickly if you're under stress.
3. Slow down when you're overly enthusiastic about something.

Beware of solving problems too quickly because of time pressure

To see how this can create horrendous problems for us, let's examine a hypothetical business situation, and see what can go wrong when decisions are made under time pressure:

CASE STUDY

You're the president of a 140-store chain of sporting good stores, most of them west of the Mississippi and in the Northeast. Although it's a competitive business, it's going well. You're in the middle of a large expansion program, business is good, the sun is shining, the birds are singing, and you're feeling great—until your vice president of finance comes to you and says, "We've got a real cash flow problem. It's February the 15th and we've just had the worst ski season in the last 25 years. Hardly any resort in the country opened up before Christmas, and with so little snow, it's been a disaster all across the nation. We've got a 10-million-dollar excess inventory in ski equipment. We can't make the interest payment on the 50-million-dollar expansion loan that's due tomorrow, and the bank won't extend it. What are you going to do?"

If the last words a pilot always says before his plane crashes are "Oh, no!" then the last words a company president speaks before his company crashes must be "Why wasn't I told?"

This turns out to be a little problem that just kept on growing, until it became a monstrous problem. Your ski buyer is one of the best in the industry. He cleverly inserted a weasel clause into all his contracts, so he could cancel or renegotiate in the event of poor snow. That's fine, and because of the bad snow conditions, he planned to take advantage of it.

However, the night before he planned to cancel the orders, he got arrested for drunk driving, and called in with the flu. Preoccupied with his problems, he missed the deadline to cancel. Because he was covering up his arrest, he didn't tell anybody. He lit candles in every church he passed, though he wasn't Catholic, and wore his knees out, praying for late snow to bail him out. It never came. Now it's so late in the season that a clearance sale wouldn't generate enough cash to pay for the advertising.

The president tells the CFO, "I need time to think about it."

He says, "You don't have time! You've got to do something now! If we don't make the three-million-dollar loan payment tomorrow, the bank will call the loan into default. The financial papers will pick it up on the first-quarter projections and our stock is going to drop in half. Let me remind you, that would mean a personal loss in net worth to you of more than $15 million."

That's the kind of real-world situation for which they don't prepare you in business college: the major decision that has to be made under time pressure, when you've pushed all the chips into the middle of the table.

Under time pressure we make several mistakes:

1. **We attempt to speed decisions by getting less input.** We rush to accounts receivable to see what cash we can bring in fast. However, we're in such a hurry that we don't check the accounts payable.

   There, we'd find we hadn't yet paid for three million dollars worth of the ski equipment. They cut the check and charged it against the books, but didn't mail it yet.

   That information might be all we need to solve the problem. I'll tell you why in a minute.

2. **We analyze information less thoroughly.** We might assume the ski inventory is scattered around the country, in our stores. That's where it's supposed to be, on February 15th. Given more time, we'd have found most of it sitting in a warehouse in Oakland.

   That information would expand our options. We could ship it to New Zealand in time for their ski season, or have a clearance sale at the warehouse. In one location, the advertising costs would be much less.

3. **We overlook important information.** We may forget the drawing for a ski trip to Argentina that we held last spring. That gave us an e-mail database of 5,000 Bay Area ski customers. Within 48 hours we could e-mail out a sale notice to them.

4. **We tend to slim down the list of possible alternatives.** One option may be renegotiating the lease payments of the stores to improve cash flow. If the bank saw we were doing that, they might renegotiate the loan.

    However, under time pressure, we dismiss it. "We've got 140 different landlords," you say. "We don't have time to go to them all."

5. **We tend to consult with fewer experts.** We may know that Charlie over at Universal Sports had this happen to him once. If we could get him on the phone, he may be a big help to us. However, Charlie is scuba diving in Belize and can't be reached, so we dismiss that possibility. If we had more time, we'd track Charlie down, or find somebody else at his company who knew how the problem was resolved.

6. **We tend to get fewer people involved in the problem-solving process.** "We don't have time for an executive committee meeting," you're thinking. "I've got to earn my pay and make a bold decision now." With more time, we might get some very valuable insights by getting the regional managers involved in a conference call.

7. **We tend to jump at the first solution that looks right.** Now it's 11:00 at night and everybody's thrashed. Your office is a sea of computer printouts and empty pizza boxes. Your executive vice president is saying, "I hate to do this, but it looks as though we're going to have to close a bunch of stores. Here's what we should do. Call a press conference in the morning and announce that we're closing the 40 least-productive stores. With that, the bank will renegotiate the loan. The stock analysts will love it, and our stock probably will go up $10 dollars a share overnight."

You say, "But that would be a debacle, half our top store managers would jump ship in the panic. You know they've been approached by headhunters as it is. Besides, we'd ruin the relationships we worked so hard to build with our suppliers!"

"Would you rather file a Chapter Thirteen? That would hold off the creditors and give us some breathing room."

"I'll never do that," you sigh. "Let's call the press conference. Which stores are we going to close?"

Because you solved the problem under time pressure, it was a bad decision. If you had spent more time, you'd have done better. You'd have learned about the negotiating leverage that existed, because you hadn't yet paid the ski suppliers. You could have gone to the supplier and negotiated a deal where they'd cancel the three-million-dollar invoice, rebilling you on September 1st. Then you arrange a massive pre-season ski sale at the San Francisco Convention Center, for Labor Day weekend. You move the merchandise into a separate corporation that you set up, which gives you collateral against which to borrow, and frees up the pressure on your existing inventory.

And because this is a fantasy, we might as well make it a good one. The Labor Day sale is such a huge success, the following year you hold pre-season clearance sales in convention centers across the nation. You promote the event on cable TV, with the show hosted by the nation's top ski racers. It becomes the most successful event in sporting goods history.

That's the way it should have gone, but instead it all went down the tubes—because you tried to solve the problem under time pressure.

Beware of being overzealous. Have the patience to understand that making the right choice may take time.

Examine the possibility of going with a temporary solution, rather than committing to a long-term answer. What would give you breathing room?

If you are forced to make a rash decision, be sure that when the pressure's off, you take another look at the problem. See if there aren't additional solutions.

When you're forced to make a decision under time pressure, you're usually better off to defer the decision, until you feel comfortable making it—in spite of the pressure you're under. It isn't always the right thing to do, but it's the right thing to do enough of the time, to make it a good rule.

Don't make choices quickly when you're under stress

I learned the second rule the hard way: I don't make decisions if I'm angry, if I'm depressed, or if I'm not feeling well. That rule has so often served me well. For instance, I'll be driving down to my office just boiling over with anger at a secretary. I can't believe she's made this mistake for the 10th time, and I feel like storming in there and reading her the riot act until she quits. Then I remember I'm not feeling good that day. Perhaps I'm coming down with something, or I'm tired because I've just come off a long speaking tour. I back off, and say to myself, "I'll take another look at this tomorrow, and see if I still feel the same way." I've never regretted being cautious like that.

If you're angry, depressed, or not feeling well, just learn to cool it. Just calm down, let some time go by, and see how you feel about it the next day. When you look back at it, you usually say to yourself, "Wow, I'm glad I didn't make any choices when I was feeling the way I did yesterday."

Slow down when you're overly enthusiastic about something

Rule number three shows that feeling too good can also be a detriment. At my company we have a standard line when we find we've made a bad choice: "Wow, you must have been feeling good when you made that decision." If you feel really good about something, slow down—because enthusiasm can blind you. If it feels too good to be true, it probably is too good to be true.

The time for enthusiasm is after you've made the decision, not before. Once you've made the decision, then your enthusiasm can sometimes make even a poor choice work. But enthusiasm before you make a decision is inviting disaster.

➡ **Key point from this chapter**

▸ Beware of solving problems too quickly because of time pressure.

▸ Don't make choices quickly if you're under stress.

▸ Slow down when you're overly enthusiastic about something.

*Indecision may
or may not be my
problem.*

— Jimmy Buffett

Chapter 14
Don't Solve Problems
Too Slowly

Now let's consider the second barrier to good problem solving: acting too slowly, which can be just as much of a problem as moving too quickly. There are six reasons why we sometimes delay a choice past the critical point:

Reason one: Defensive avoidance

I believe psychologists when they say that everyone has a built-in defensive avoidance of problems. In layperson's language, that means we avoid problems and move toward opportunities. In problem solving this psychological desire to move away from problems causes three attitudes that slow the decision-making process:

1. It can't happen to me.
2. I can take care of it later.
3. Let somebody else worry about it.

The first attitude is: This can't happen to me. Sure, 10 restaurants have gone out of business at this location, but they weren't doing what I'm going to do. I 'm not going to let that happen to me.

The second attitude is: I can take care of it later. Rather than recognizing we have a problem that needs a solution, we tend to think, "I've lots of other things to do, and this can wait." It doesn't occur to us that we're procrastinating because the other things are much more fun.

And the third attitude that comes from defensive avoidance is the attitude of "let somebody else worry about it." If you're the president of your company, that's a disastrous attitude to take and one you strongly need to resist. When you're the one running the company, the buck stops with you. Unless you're actively making things happen, the inertia that's built into any organization will take over.

Reason two: A "don't fix it unless it's broke" attitude

The second reason for acting too slowly is being satisfied with what you've got. These days, the "don't fix it unless it's broke" attitude can sink you. In today's fast moving business environment you must anticipate that it's going to break. This translates into: It isn't always going to be a best-seller, so improve it before its sales peak.

Gillette was riding high in 1990. They were the market leader in both disposable and cartridge razors by a three-to-one margin. Even so, they spent $200 million to develop the Sensor razor and an additional $175 million to advertise it. That's far more than all their profits from the previous year. They had every justification for saying "Let's not fix it, because it isn't broken." But they know you can't get away with that for very long in today's business environment. Never become satisfied with what you've got...always be improving.

Reason three: An obsession with brainstorming

The third reason for acting too slowly on a decision is an obsessive desire to involve other people in the problem-solving process. Brainstorming can be a very valuable aid to good problem solving, but don't let it delay the decision too much. If a decision must be made, set a deadline for making it. Get as many people involved as you can, but not if it delays the decision too much. Unless something significant comes up to make you change the deadline, go for it. If you still can't get a consensus and the deadline is near, let the manager closest to the problem make the decision.

In Section Seven of this book, you'll find a whole section on when and if you should brainstorm a problem.

Reason four: Gathering too much information

Too much information is a real threat in today's world. We have access to so much information, we easily become confused. It becomes like a mental noise that blocks intuitive thinking.

Be careful that your Internet searches are not too vague. If you Google a question and get 975,000 answers, your search terms are way too broad. You can drown in too much information.

Be cautious about storing information. Before you print something out and file it, say to yourself, "Do I really need to have a hard copy of this, or can I access the information on my computer if I need to see it again?

The Pentagon has long dreamed of digitizing all its records, just like your medical group did years ago. They haven't been able to do it because they are drowning in too much information. Even the Secretary of Defense said that, "Trying to get information from the Pentagon is like trying to drink out of a fire hose."

Reason five: Attempting to predict the future

The fifth reason for slow problem solving is time wasted in attempts to predict the future. Even economists can't predict the future.

Economists fail in their predictions, because they won't accept that people are well-informed, rational creatures who'll always do what's in their best interest. Every other business runs on that assumption, but economists refuse to factor it in.

My conclusion about all this? Futurism is fascinating, but rarely accurate. Take hydrogen-fueled cars for example. We've been hearing for 30 years that hydrogen cars will clean the air rather than pollute it, but where are they? In 1965 Herbert Simon, a leading expert in artificial intelligence, predicted that by 1985 machines would be able to do anything a human could do. No sign of that yet.

Remember the prediction that once there was a computer in every home that all our traffic problems would go away? Futurists were convinced that most people would work from a workstation in their home. Not only would our traffic problems go away but there would be a huge population shift from the cities to the countryside as people realized that they no longer had to go to work every day. What happened to that idea?

How relevant are predictions to your business anyway? It's far better to monitor what's going on and react to it, than to waste time trying to predict what might happen.

Reason six: A fear of failure

The sixth reason for making decisions too slowly is an obvious one: fear of failure. Keep reminding yourself that you can't win if you're afraid of losing.

The best way I know to avoid the fear of losing is to figure out the worst-case scenario. What's the worst thing that could happen if you make a wrong decision? It's probably not as bad as you fear. Remember: The only person qualified to tell you that something won't work, is a person who has tried it and found that it didn't work! There are a million people out there running around telling you that things won't work, but when you check their expertise, they don't have much. They're telling you it won't work and yet they've never attempted it themselves. My rule is: Nobody's entitled to tell me I can't do something unless they've done it and failed.

➦ Key points from this chapter

There are six reasons why we might solve a problem too slowly:

▶ Defensive avoidance. We have built in psychological mechanism that encourages us to avoid problems.

▶ A "don't fix it unless it's broke" attitude. Anticipating that what you're doing now, won't always be the best thing to do, keeps you one step ahead of the competition.

▶ An obsession with brainstorming. Participatory involvement is great, but not if it delays the decision too much. Set a deadline, and when it comes, go with the best available solution.

▶ Gathering too much information. Don't let it bury you!

▶ Wasting time trying to predict the future.

▶ A fear of failure.

Chapter 15

How Quickly Should You Choose?

How quickly should you move on your problem? Sometimes the need to make a choice overrides all the rules about *how* to solve the problem. When that happens, you have to go with the best input you've got, and the best minds you have available at that time. But knowing when you have to move fast, rather than taking the time to make a more perfect decision, is a fine art. There are four urgency factors that tell you how quickly you have to move:

The first urgency factor: What's the competition doing?

In business, knowing what the competition is doing is essential to knowing how fast you have to move. If you've got an exclusive patent on a new genetically engineered drug, you may have months or years in which to solve the problems that come up. You can take the time to get everything just right before you move. In the computer business you may have only days to make a move.

Knowing the competition is the key, but how do you get information on what the competition's doing? First, don't be afraid to ask. Unless it violates fair trade rules, just pick up the phone and ask. Now, they may not answer the question, but a good reporter knows there are many more reasons to ask a question, other than the hope the person might give you an answer. You can learn a lot by studying the way people respond. Reporters constantly ask questions that they know the person will not answer. They want to know *how* the person refuses to answer the question and how he reacts to being asked. Ask and you still gather information, even if you don't get an answer.

I was once the dinner speaker at the annual meeting of a large packaging company. At dinner, they sat me between the president of the packaging company and the vice president of their biggest customer, a Fortune 100 company. I said to the president of the packaging company on my left, "How much of these people's business do you get?"

He told me, "We don't know—they wouldn't tell us that. We just know they don't like to give all their packaging business to one company."

A few minutes later, I turned to the vice president, who was their biggest customer, and said, "How much of your packaging business do these people get?"

To my astonishment he told me, "27.8 percent."

I said, "I suppose you like to spread your business around?"

He said, "Well, that used to be our policy, but we recently changed that. Now if we find a supplier that's willing to partner with us, we're willing to give them all our business."

Here was valuable information the man on my left would've loved to have—and could have had. But he didn't ask, because he didn't think they'd answer the question. The moral of the story? Ask the question even if you are sure they won't answer.

When you talk to a competitor, if you want to get, you've got to give. Be ready to horse trade information. Sometimes it's best to volunteer the information first, which obligates them to reciprocate.

"But that doesn't make sense," you say. "I don't want to give my competition any information." Well, I can see where that may be so. Just be smart about the way you do it. Don't call or go to see the competition yourself. Send somebody who doesn't know your secrets. Then when they're asked for information you don't want to give away, they can honestly say, "I'm sorry, I just don't know. I'd tell you if I did, but I don't." In that way you only have to trade the information you want to trade.

Knowing what the competition is doing relates to your personal life as well as your business life. You're wondering whether you have the courage to ask out that beautiful woman, who just broke up with her significant other. She's gorgeous, to die for—enough to make bishop kick out a stained glass window, as Raymond Chandler would say. And she just won 10 million dollars in the state lottery. You've probably got a lot of competition that is ready to move quickly! You'd better get on the phone and do it now, or you'll regret it for the rest of your life.

The first factor that tells you how much time you have to make the decision is what the competition is doing.

The second urgency factor: The life cycle of the decision

Sometimes, if you wait too long, it's too late—however good the solution to your problem. If your decision has a short life cycle, you need to make a decision faster. What businesspeople all over the country are telling me, is this: In today's speeded-up economy, decisions need to be made faster, because their life cycle is so much shorter.

Take the now famous case of U.S. Airways pilot "Sulley" Sullenberger flying from La Guardia airport in New York to Charlotte, North Carolina. Shortly after takeoff he hit a large flock of Canadian geese that disabled both his engines, something that very rarely happens. He had a massive problem on his hands and only seconds to solve it. He discussed with air traffic control the possibility of returning to La Guardia or trying to land at Teterboro Airport in New Jersey. That must have been the shortest brainstorming session in history. He quickly decided that his only viable option was to ditch the Airbus A320 in the Hudson River. Not an attractive option to be sure, because this was January 15th and the water was extremely cold.

Note the way in which he solved his problem. He methodically eliminated what wouldn't work and narrowed his options down to what had a possibility of working. He narrowed his options, not expecting to find the perfect solution. I wonder how many times in his decades of piloting he thought, "What would I do now if I lost both engines?"

His fast problem-solving skills saved the life of all 155 people on board. It turned out that if this had to happen it couldn't have happened with a more qualified pilot on board. He had flown F4s for the U.S. Air Force before spending 29 years as a commercial pilot for U.S. Airways. He had founded a company focused on helping businesses improve safety.

In spite of all this specialized knowledge of disaster situations and his impressive piloting experience, he said in a CBS *60 Minutes* interview that the moments before the crash were "the worst sickening, pit-of-your-stomach, falling-through-the-floor feeling" that he had ever experienced.

It was a historic event in which the urgent need to solve the problem met the most experienced and talented problem solver on the planet. When that happens you don't have or need much time to come up with a perfect solution.

My good friend Mike Summey, who was my coauthor on the *Weekend Millionaire* series of books, and owns and pilots a Beechcraft King Air airplane, added an additional insight to the Sulley Sullenberger incident. He told me that it's one thing to choose a solution quickly to your problem. The key is that, having chosen a solution, it enables you to focus solely on making that solution work. Sulley made a quick decision to put the plane in the river, and once that decision was made he was able to focus all his attention on making a good landing on the water.

Had he hesitated over his decision, he may have gotten out of position to reach the river and no level of piloting skill would have averted a disaster.

The third urgency factor: How reversible is the decision?

This means: If you goof, how easily can you get out of trouble? Perhaps your banker has called you and said, "I can't believe the real estate opportunity we have for you. We've just foreclosed on an office building that would be an ideal headquarters for your company. If you can make a decision by noon tomorrow, you can get it for 50 percent of the true market value, and we'll finance it 100 percent."

If you're a good problem solver, the question isn't "Would this make a good main office for us?" That might take you weeks to decide. Rather, the question is. "If I go ahead, how reversible is the decision?" If you truly can buy it for 50 percent of the market value, and they'll finance it 100 percent, you can't lose. Even if you never move into the building, you can sell it, and probably make a very good profit. To me, that's a decision that shouldn't take more than five minutes to make, even if it's a multimillion-dollar investment. Provided, of course, you know enough about the current real estate market. And provided your corporate mission statement supports such a move.

Reversibility is a concept of which we all ought to be more conscious. Before you do anything you should be thinking, "How reversible is this action?" Slamming the front door of your house or the door of your car is not a problem because if you have the key in your pocket you can quickly reverse the action. If the only key is inside the car or house it could create a big problem.

Whenever you choose a solution to a problem you should be thinking, "This seems like the right thing to do, but if I'm wrong can I easily undo the action?"

The fourth urgency factor: How big is the downside?

What's the loss potential if you make the wrong decision? We all fall into this trap. We agonize over which video to rent. We should be saying, "What am I spending time on this for? The down side is only $3.00. I'll get this one too. If I decide not to watch it, I've lost $3.00. That's tipping money, so it's no big deal."

I remember very clearly standing in the streets of Pamplona, Spain, with my son John, who wanted to run with the bulls. His motto is "It's better to be gored than bored." I wanted to run with the bulls, too—mainly because it would make a terrific story for my talks! But if a bull tossed me, my speaker friends would never let me get over it. When a bull tosses a speaker, it's like a man biting a dog: It's headline news!

When I evaluated the upside versus the downside, the risk didn't make sense. The upside was very small, and the downside huge. I wouldn't have to be tossed by a bull for it to be a disaster, either. After we left Spain, we were going to the Alps to climb Mont Blanc and the Matterhorn. Just a twisted ankle would bring that plan to a screeching halt. My son was 21 years old. If worse came to worst, he had a couple of decades left to climb those mountains. I was 50 years old, so I didn't have many years left when I could throw myself at the Matterhorn and have a chance of getting to the top. That's what we call a small upside and a huge downside!

➨ Key points from this chapter

▶ Sometimes you're forced to make a decision without having the time to go through all the stages of problem solving. Here are the urgency factors that tell you when you must move fast:

1. First, what's the competition doing? If you're in a race to see who can get to market first, you may be better off to go with what you've got.

2. Second, how long is the life cycle of the decision? The decision to marry someone should take longer than the decision to market a new Christmas toy.

3. Third, how reversible is the decision? If you goof, can you get out of it without too much damage?

4. And fourth, what's the downside? If you can absorb the loss, vacillating may cost more than writing off a mistake.

▶ What if you've considered all these points, and they're still pressuring you for a decision before you're ready? The rule is that you're probably better off to defer making a decision. It isn't a 100 percent rule. But it's the best thing to do enough of the time to make it a good rule.

▶ If you're forced to make a decision, do it, and then focus on making that decision work.

> *If you owe the bank $100, that's your problem.*
> *If you owe the bank $100 million, that's the bank's problem.*
>
> —J. Paul Getty

Chapter 16

If the Horse Drops Dead, Get Off Fast

Kenny Rogers told us years ago, "You've got to know when to hold 'em, know when to fold 'em." Some of the smartest businesspeople I know have fallen into the trap of being unwilling to pull the plug on a decision to which they're committed.

The are four reasons why we are reluctant to admit that the horse is dead:

1. Admitting failure will ruin my image or my company's image.
2. Failing to accept the situation as it exists today.
3. Deciding up-front that failure is unthinkable.
4. I have too much invested in this to walk away.

Admitting failure will ruin my image or my company's image

Don't think that way. A smart businessperson doesn't feel that filing Chapter Thirteen bankruptcy is unthinkable if it's the only way he or she can save the company. If General Motors can go into bankruptcy and emerge stronger than before, it might be the right thing for you to do, too.

Failing to accept the situation as it exists today

A smart problem solver learns to deal with what's happening now—not what happened yesterday, not what might have happened today if everybody had done what they were supposed to do, but what's happening now. Being upset and angry with people who have let you down doesn't solve problems. Accepting the realism of the moment and moving forward is what solves problems.

Let's say you're climbing a mountain and the rope breaks. Ropes are not supposed to break like that. When you find yourself stranded on a narrow ledge with a broken ankle, it's okay to curse the manufacturer of the rope—but only for a while. After a few minutes, it becomes counter-productive behavior. The sooner you get past that and start dealing with the existing situation, the better off you'll be.

Deciding up front that failure is unthinkable

Don't get too personally committed to your plan. You can ride that plan into oblivion if you're not careful. Sure, you've made a choice and you want to get behind it all the way. Yet, to be 100 percent committed to making it work is deadly. You may be riding the horse in the right direction, but if it drops dead, get off as quickly as you possibly can.

I have too much invested in this to walk away

In negotiating presentations I teach that the longer you can keep someone in a negotiation, the more chance you have of getting what you want.

The problem is that the same principle works on you, too. The longer you are in a negotiation the more likely you are to make concessions. Why does it work that way? Because your subconscious mind is now screaming at you, "You can't walk away from this empty-handed after the time and effort you've spent on it. You have to be able to make it work."

When solving a problem you should disregard any time or money that you have already invested in a project. That time and money are gone whether you strike a deal or not. Always look at things as they exist at that moment and think, "Disregarding all the time and money we've poured into this deal up to now, should we go ahead?"

Never be reluctant to pull the plug if it doesn't make sense anymore. It's much cheaper to write off your investment than it is to plow ahead with a deal that isn't right for you just because you have so much invested in it.

That's one of the things that makes Donald Trump such a powerful negotiator: He's not afraid to pull the plug on a deal that no longer makes sense. For example, he spent $100 million to acquire the site for Television City on the West Side of Manhattan. He spent millions more designing plans that would include a 150-story tower, the world's tallest at the time, and a magnificent television studio to which he hoped to attract NBC. However, when he couldn't negotiate the right tax concessions from the city, he shelved the entire project, because what was a great investment five years before and a good investment a year before became a poor investment in the current real estate market. He put the entire project on hold, hoping that the market would improve, which it eventually did.

You have to solve your problems in the same way. Forget what you've already invested and examine whether it still looks good the way things stand now.

One more thing about killing a project: If someone in your organization initiated a project, don't let that person have the final say on pulling the plug. He or she may be too emotionally involved with the decision to be objective. If he or she is reluctant to pull the plug, move the decision to someone who isn't emotionally involved.

Sure it's wonderful to say to yourself, "I'm going to make this solution work even if it kills me." Just don't let it kill you. Be realistic enough to realize that you've made a mistake. Correct the problem and get back on track as quickly as you can.

➡ Key points from this chapter

▶ Don't let your pride stop you from pulling the plug on projects that aren't working.

▶ A smart businessperson will file Chapter Thirteen bankruptcy if it's the only way he or she can save the company.

▶ If other people caused your problems it's okay to get angry with them, but only for a while. You have to deal with the problem.

▶ Don't get too personally committed to your plan.

▶ Forget about the time and money it has taken you to get to this point. Your only consideration should be what is the smart thing to do from this point on.

▶ Be realistic enough to realize that you've made a mistake. Correct the problem and get back on track as quickly as you can.

Chapter 17
Don't Bang Your Head Against Concrete Principles

Do you ever get the feeling you're the only person in the world who can see the solution to a complicated social problem?

"I know how to solve the drug problem in Mexico," you think. All we have to do is change the currency. Just eliminate all the present U.S. dollars, make it worthless, and then replace it with a new currency. Countries change currency all the time, but usually when they want to devalue the currency. Why wouldn't it work for drugs? When the European countries ditched the franc, the mark and the lira for the euro, what did the drug dealers do with all the cash that they had accumulated?

Sounds like a good idea, right? However, there's a concrete principle involved that makes that an awful idea: Because the moment you attempt to replace the dollar, the economy would be ruined by hyperinflation, as everybody with existing dollars tries to convert them into goods and services.

Or perhaps it occurs to you that the solution to all our energy problems is to devise a system that transmits electricity to automobiles through the air, the same way radio waves or television signals are transmitted. Unfortunately there are some concrete principles involved that simply say "That won't work because..." Scientists have been trying to develop this for decades and still haven't been able to light up a 100-watt light bulb from 5 feet away.

Perhaps your problem is that you've been laid off from your job and are too old to get another one. After much fretting you decide that the best thing to do is move to Australia. "They have cradle to grave welfare state," a friend told you once. "They'll take care of you." It might be a good idea to call the Australian consulate and find out how hard it is to get a permanent resident visa. You may find that it's almost impossible.

Don't give up on these flights of fancy, however. Kick them around for a while and see if they produce a great idea that would work. When analytical thinking tells you that replacing the currency will cause hyperinflation, you now understand why it won't work, but maybe something similar would solve the problem. When you learn that the law of physics stops you from transmitting electricity like a radio wave, you should always think, "Maybe that's so, but let's kick it around for a while and perhaps that will stimulate a different solution."

➡ Key points from this chapter

▸ When you think you've found the perfect answer check it out to be sure that there are no concrete principles that make it impossible.

▸ Even if you find your solution won't work because of a concrete principle, don't give up. A little creative thinking might produce a workable solution.

Intuitive Problem Solving

*Intuition becomes increasingly
valuable in the new information society
precisely because there is
so much data.*

—John Naisbitt

Wouldn't it be wonderful to be that one person in a million who appears to have a sure-fire, never-miss, intuition? C.R. Smith, the first president of American Airlines, seemed to have it. He'd never worked at an airline before, but he just seemed to have a feel for it. For example, on his first day on the job he ordered a change in pilots' uniforms that became the standard to this day.

After one flight in a DC-2, he called up Donald Douglas, the head of Douglas Aircraft, who made the plane. He said, "Don, I want you to expand this plane, so it'll carry 21 passengers in the daytime, and sleep 14 at night." Douglas told him he was crazy, that his suggestion wouldn't work. Smith wouldn't give in. He kept Douglas on the phone for two hours. He promised to buy 20 of the planes on the spot. Finally Douglas agreed to have one of his engineers take another look at it. The improvements Smith suggested resulted in the most successful plane in aviation history, the DC-3.

Once, he virtually ignored a foot-high study the company had done on swapping routes with Pan Am. Instead, he simply walked over to Pan Am President Bill Seawall's office and made the swap.

The company once spent $100,000 on a study to cool airplanes. Their recommendation? Paint the planes white. Smith wouldn't even read the study. "Forget it," he said, "If you want to cool them, find some other way." It led to the air conditioning that we enjoy today.

Intuitive hunches are fascinating things

Going against the advice of his father and all the experts in the oil industry, Nelson Bunker Hunt played a hunch he could find oil in Libya. He drilled into the Sarir field, which turned out to be one of the largest reserves of oil on the planet. Soon he was pumping $100,000 of oil a day, and his hunch made him $16 billion. But intuition can desert you also. Soon Moammar Gadhafi nationalized the oil industry in Libya and then Hunt lost most of his fortune in an ill-timed attempt to corner the silver market.

Gustave Leven, a Paris stockbroker, tried to find a buyer for an almost-defunct company that bottled spring water. Although the French show little interest in drinking water of any kind, he bought the company himself, on a hunch. Part of it was fascination with the unusual shape of the bottles, fashioned after the Indian clubs with which the eccentric English founder of the company exercised. Gustave Leven went on to build Perrier into a billion-dollar company.

Conrad Hilton claimed he built his hotel empire on hunches. When he bought the corporate assets of the Stevens Hotel in Chicago, he submitted a bid for $165,000. "Then somehow that didn't seem right to me," he said. "Another figure kept coming, $180,000. It satisfied me. It seemed fair. It felt right. I changed my bid to the larger figure on that hunch. When the bids were opened, the closest bid to mine was $179,800. I got the Stevens Corporation by a narrow margin of $200. Eventually those assets returned to me two million."

Jonas Salk said: "Intuition is my partner, I wake up every morning to see what gifts it will toss me." Bach used to say the problem wasn't in finding melodies, but avoiding stepping on them when he got out of bed.

Earl Nightingale said, "Ideas are elusive, slippery things. Best to keep a pad of paper, and a pencil at your bed side, so you can stab them during the night, before they get away." To that I would add: "Intuition is like a deer nuzzling your sleeping bag on a chilly October morning. Don't be startled by it, or you'll scare it away."

In this section, we'll explore intuitive problem solving. You'll learn that intuition is not magic; it's a skill that can be learned. I'll show you how.

> *Sometimes the situation is only a problem because it is looked at in a certain way. Looked at in another way, the right course of action may be so obvious that the problem no longer exists.*
>
> —Edward de Bono

Chapter 18
Do You Have a Golden Gut?

Generating intuition may come naturally to you, or you may have to work at it. To find out how naturally intuitive you are, let's take the Golden Gut Test. I'm going to ask you 15 questions. See how many of these sound as though they describe you.

True   False   1. I think the best way to learn new computer software is to install it and play with it for a while. Later, I read the instructions.

True   False   2. I should be allowed to set my own work hours. I know when I perform best and it's not necessarily the same hours each day.

True   False   3. People think my desk is a mess, but I know where things are.

True   False   4. I think of myself as an honest and moral person, but sometimes I'm still not sure I'm doing the right thing. But that's okay.

True   False   5. When the evidence tells me I should decide one way, but I've a strange feeling I shouldn't, I usually follow my feelings.

True   False   6. When I don't have precise directions to get somewhere, it doesn't bother me. I'll go to the general area, and ask somebody the way.

True   False   7. I like problem solving because it gives me a chance to play with possibilities.

True   False   8. I get bored easily.

True   False   9. I'll listen to expert advice, but don't always follow it.

True   False   10. I know a lot of people who play their hunches.

True   False   11. I like novels, as well as non-fiction books.

True   False   12. Multiple answer questions are not very effective, so students should have to give essay answers.

True   False   13. No one ever accused me of being a detail person.

True   False   14. Making an appointment for a precise day and time ties me down.

True   False   15. I enjoy taking risks.

Total number of "True" answers: _____

Let's see how you did on that. Here are the Golden Gut test score results:

Twelve or more true answers.

You have a 24-carat golden gut. I suggest you follow your hunches whether you think they're right or not.

Nine to eleven.

You have an 18-carat golden gut. Trust but verify your hunches.

Six to eight.

You have a brass gut. You sometimes get good hunches but don't trust them yet. You need this book to help you develop your intuition.

Less than six.

You have a lead gut. You do everything by analysis and almost never take chances.

What was the Golden Gut Test all about? It was a test of your ability to function, and even relish, a world that's not totally logical. Human beings have an incredible desire to know what's going on. You can put a cow in a field, and it will stay in that field all its life and never wonder what's happening on the other side of the hill. Human beings will spend billions to find out if there is microscopic life on Mars. We've simply got to know and understand what's going on.

Intuition comes in four ways:

1. **A gut reaction.** You may have research that urges you to go one way but you still feel strongly that you should go the other way.

2. **Intellectual.** The answer to a problem suddenly pops into your head.

3. **Spiritual.** A sudden revelation that clarifies your relationship with your universe. My favorite word is grace, meaning that feeling of oneness with God and the universe. Amazing grace, as Christians sing.

4. **Alarm.** That sudden feeling of danger that guides you and protects you.

Your ability to develop intuition is in direct relationship to your ability to accept this truth: Sometimes you can figure out why things happen, and sometimes there just isn't any way you can figure it out.

The ability to work with ambiguity makes you a better problem solver, and it makes you a better businessperson. Not every problem offers a perfect solution. Be willing to make mistakes, and be willing to let your people make mistakes.

Joel Bruckner, professor of management at Columbia Business School, says, "The need to prove we're right, overwhelms our ability to think rationally. It blinds you to the early warning signals that a project is failing and creates false hope of a turnaround."

Be sure you're letting your people know that it's okay to make mistakes. Perhaps one of the reasons Johnson and Johnson has been so successful, is the story CEO James Burke loves to tell about his early days with the company. He had spearheaded a project to market a chest rub for children. It died a horrible death in the marketplace. He was called in front of the company's chairman, General Robert Wood Johnson, who said, "Are you the person who cost us all that money?"

"Yes sir," he fumbled, feeling sure he was about to get fired.

"I just wanted to congratulate you," the General said. "If you're making mistakes, it means you're making decisions and taking risks. We won't grow unless you take risks."

Your ability to develop a golden gut is in direct relationship to your willingness to accept that when you make a decision, you open the door to ambiguity. The door I want you to walk through is the door from a logical world in which everything can be explained—into the room of intuition. Where things can happen without your understanding why. Where you move ahead with confidence to solve your problem, even though you don't have every assurance that you're doing the right thing.

Pure intuition is like a photographic memory. It would be great to have one. It would make life a lot simpler. You can develop it by learning how to saturate your mind with information, so that your brain begins to chunk information. That enables you to access huge amounts of information quickly and easily. Then develop the intense focus of an Isaac Newton. Finally, train yourself to deal with ambiguity, because you can't be intuitive if you insist on perfection before you feel confident about solving the problem.

➡ Key points from this chapter

▶ Use the Golden Gut Test to determine how intuitive you are.

▶ Sometimes you can figure out why things happen, and sometimes there just isn't any way you can figure it out.

▶ Intuition comes in four forms: a gut reaction, intellectual intuition, spiritual intuition, and alarm.

▶ The ability to work with ambiguity makes you a better problem solver.

▶ Be willing to make mistakes, and don't censure your employees who make mistakes trying to come up with new ideas.

▶ Improve your intuition by chunking information.

Chapter 19

Is Intuitive Problem Solving Obsolete?

In many ways it seems that in America we have moved away from intuitive problem solving and become obsessed with logic. That's a shame because it means we've turned our back on what made us great.

One of the reasons we've moved away from intuitive thought is that we feel its usefulness has been supplanted by scientific thought, which is rooted in logic. In the Western world, scientific discovery has been so astonishingly successful for us that we put intuitive thought on the back burner.

Is intuition still relevant as a problem-solving tool?

The stream of scientific discovery that started in the 17th century turned into a river in the 18th century, a torrent in the 19th century, and became a tumultuous roar of progress in the 20th century and first decade of the 21st century. Once we passed the millennium there was one final, enormous swing from intuitive problem solving to logical problem solving. It was fueled by two key factors: the World Wide Web, which brought us into the information age, and the move to larger and larger corporations.

When a mainframe can produce a Decision Tree or a Fault Tree in seconds, what use do we have for intuitive problem solving? A corporate systems department can now develop payoff tables that can coherently juggle a thousand different factors in minutes.

Look at the changes in the way that stocks are traded at the New York Stock Exchange. Although the cable news networks love to report from the trading floor with blue-coat traders in the background frantically waving buy/sell slips at the other traders, few trades are made that way anymore. Today, less than 30 percent of shares are traded on the floor of the exchange. Billions of shares are bought and sold every day from lighting-fast computers without any human input. Those super computers can trade thousands of orders per second.

Traders still start shaking when you mention what happened on May 6, 2010. A mutual funds computer erroneously dumped $4.1 billion of securities on the market. Within minutes the high-frequency traders' computers snapped them up. The stock market dropped 600 points in 15 minutes. The incident became known as the Flash Crash. Since then the SEC has set up circuit breakers that prevent trading in any stock that drops more than 10 percent in five minutes.

In a world where super computers make decisions at lightning speeds, isn't it an anachronism to have an expensive executive sitting behind a closed door waiting for intuition to inspire him in a blinding flash of light? Probably.

Except that scientists are frequently wrong. In fact, there have been two major themes dominating scientific thought during the last 50 years, and both of them are directly related to problem solving. Both of them turned out to be wrong.

Two questionable scientific theories

First, consider reductionism. Scientists became obsessed with the thought that if they could understand how the smallest component of the universe worked, then they'd know everything. University of Michigan professor John Holland says that the idea is that you could understand the world, all of nature, by examining smaller and smaller pieces of it. When assembled, the small pieces would explain the whole.

That might work if you're trying to understand how a watch works, but in nature there doesn't seem to be a smallest component. Even scientists can't comprehend the smallest picture any more than they can grasp the huge picture: what's beyond the universe. They used to think that the atom was the smallest element. Then scientists found that atoms consist of protons, electrons, and neutrons. Now they don't know. The best they can say is that matter isn't comprised of molecules of solid atoms. It's an intricate web of something they can only describe as energy.

Second, consider Universal Predictability, which is the belief that everything is predictable. It is the belief that computers, by their incredible ability to process huge amounts of information, would make human problem solving obsolete. Back in the 1960s, scientists began combining the basic laws of physics with the incredible computing power of the mainframe, to make remarkably precise predictions. They could send a space probe to the edge of the universe and predict its course with unbelievable accuracy. Suddenly they could create robotic factories that would manufacture complex or miniature items with almost no chance of error, because they could predict any problem and compensate for it.

It was then that scientists began to believe in Universal Predictability: that if they could generate enough information and process it through a big enough mainframe fast enough, they could eliminate the need for guesswork. All problems could be solved with computers. They'd never make a mistake again. It turns out they got a bit carried away.

Suddenly one of them looked up from their computer and said, "If we can do all that, why didn't we know with certainty that Hurricane Katrina would destroy New Orleans? Why didn't we know that BP's oil platform in the Gulf of Mexico would explode?"

It suddenly dawned on scientists that some things are inherently unpredictable. They knew they'd goofed when they tried to make long-term weather predictions. Scientists spent $500 million on satellites and computers with the belief they could solve one of mankind's biggest problems: the unpredictable nature of weather. It turned out to be a complete waste of money. Weather is unpredictable beyond a few days. Any activity that involves nature, or human beings, is unpredictable on a long-term basis.

The chaos theory

The name given to this new theory was the chaos theory. Any small deviation from normal behavior becomes magnified as it moves through the system. If a cormorant decides to dive into the water in Central China, it affects the weather in New York. If a waitress smiles seductively at a truck driver in Des Moines, it could shut down an auto assembly plant in Tennessee. (Depending on how cute she is, of course.)

That's why you can never depend on computers to make decisions for you. Or believe in any completely logical system of analysis, however sophisticated it may be. Good problem solvers use logic as a tool, but to be a great problem solver, you must blend in the magic of intuition. If you can do that, you can empower logical decisions with the magic of intuition.

I'm going to teach you later how to analyze problems and use logical problem-solving tools, but don't lose sight of this fact: No amount of analysis will ever replace a human mind perfectly trained to access and process intuition. Logical problem solving reduces the possibility of error. Intuitive problem solving develops creative alternatives. By turning our back on old-style intuition, we're missing a great opportunity to develop new and exciting solutions to our problems.

These days we're beginning to look inward for solutions. Can we rediscover our power of intuition and put it to work for us? Intuition is an awesome power, no question about it.

However, I don't think it's a gift given to a chosen few; I think it's a skill we can all learn. I'll show you how in the next chapter.

▶ Key points from this chapter

▶ The incredible success of scientific discovery in the Western world has caused us to turn our back on intuitive discovery.

▶ Two of the great lines of scientific thought in this century have been proven wrong.

▶ Reductionism, the thought that if we can understand the smallest part of a problem, we can understand the whole.

▶ Universal Predictability, the thought that if we can input enough information into a problem, we can predict what will happen.

▶ Good problem solving is a blend of logic and intuition.

Chapter 20

How Chunking Improves Your Intuition

There are three things that limit your power of intuition:

1. Your short-term memory.

2. Your working memory.

3. Your attention span.

Intuition depends on your ability to pull together unrelated facts from your pool of knowledge and throw them at the decision.

Chunking is a weird term describing what the mind does when it stores information in parcels rather than individual pieces. Although you're bombarded by millions of bits of information, you can only comfortably juggle about seven pieces of information at one time. If you try to handle many more than seven, your mind overloads.

If you play golf, you're aware of this. There are more than seven things you have to remember to correctly swing a club. I find I can comfortably concentrate on seven of these at one time. I can think:

1. Relax.

2. Keep my head down.

3. Slow down my back swing.

4. Don't over-swing.
5. Hit through the ball.
6. Grip firmly with the left hand.
7. Follow through.

But if I'm having a bad round, I try to think of other things, too: Don't sway, keep my heel planted, and so on. And once I try thinking of more than seven things at a time, my game goes south. I have a terrible time trying to concentrate on all those things at once.

How do you ever learn a game as complex as golf? You handle it by chunking information. Instead of separating the components of the swing in your mind, you chunk them together as "the swing." You probably can't describe what you're doing, but you know it feels right.

Let me give you a very simple example of chunking. Remember when you first learned to tie your shoelaces? You learned to pull both ends tight, cross them over into a simple bow, fold one loose end in half, and then...then what do you do? Did you forget? See what I mean? We no longer know what it takes to tie a shoe, because we've chunked all those individual pieces of knowledge together.

A good auto mechanic chunks everything he knows about fixing cars. I once took a car into my mechanic because it sounded as though it was falling apart. I felt sure it would take a major engine overhaul to fix it. As I pulled up, expecting the worst, he said, "You've got a loose engine mount. Give me 10 minutes and I'll fix it for you." And this was without even lifting the hood! Had he been less of an expert, he'd have gone through a series of checks before he arrived at the same conclusion.

A weather-beaten old rancher in Kansas may sit on his front porch and say, "We'll likely get some rain tomorrow." Ask him how he knows and he won't be able to tell you. He long ago chunked all he knows about weather.

People who appear to have great intuition really have become very adept at chunking information. It enables them to access huge amounts of information in microseconds. The key to intuition, then, is saturating yourself with information about the decision.

➠ Key points from this chapter

▸ Intuition springs from continuously focusing your mind on a problem or opportunity.

▸ Our minds can only handle seven pieces of information at a time. To get beyond that, we must "chunk" information.

▸ We start to create intuition when we saturate our minds with information.

> *No problem can be solved until it is reduced to some simple form. The changing of a vague difficulty into a specific, concrete form is a very essential element in thinking.*
>
> —J.P. Morgan

Chapter 21

Intuition or Rapid Reasoning?

Many inventions attributed to intuition were really not that at all. They were a result of experts who could think fast by chunking underlying knowledge. Listen to these examples and decide whether they're really intuition, or thinking fast by chunking underlying knowledge:

Art Fry first thought of Post–it notes while singing in church. His first thought was for a bookmark that wouldn't fall out, rather than something to write on. It was fortunate he worked for a company like 3M, which encourages its employees to follow up on their hunches. Lewis Lehr, the chairman of the company, says their corporate structure is "designed specifically to encourage young intrepreneurs to take an idea and run with it." He calls it the heart of their design for growth.

Louis Pasteur, a French chemist and microbiologist, was examining some fermented grapes when he suddenly realized that grapes only ferment when the skin is broken. He suddenly knew germs in the air caused bacterial infection, not spontaneous internal generation, as he previously thought. His discovery led to the saving of the French beer, wine, and silk industries, and to the process we now know as pasteurization.

When Ray Kroc tried to buy the McDonalds brothers' share of his company, they stunned him by asking for 2.7 million, an amount that would leave them a million dollars each after taxes. Kroc recalled: "I'm not a gambler and I didn't have that kind of money, but my funny bone instinct kept urging me on. I closed my office door, cussed up and down, and threw things out the window. Then I called my lawyer back and said: 'Take it!'" It was a smart move, however much it hurt. Their share would soon be worth $15 million a year to Kroc.

Alexander Fleming was about to throw away some bacteria he'd been cultivating. A mold growth was contaminating the culture. Suddenly he noticed a bacteria-free circle around the mold growth. A hunch led him to investigate it further. He found a substance in the mold that prevented growth of the bacteria even when he diluted it 800 times. He called it penicillin. Years later Fleming was given a tour of a modern research laboratory with a perfect sterile environment. His guide commented, "What a pity you didn't have a place like this to work in. Who can tell what you might have discovered?"

"Well, certainly not penicillin," Fleming laughed.

King Gillette was a salesman who sold cork that went inside bottle caps. It fascinated him. "Isn't that something?" he'd say, "I make my living selling something people throw away, and keep on re-buying. I wonder what else people would buy, throw away, and buy again?" That's when he hit upon the idea of the disposable razor blade.

All of these appear to be examples of a magical intuition, when really their expertise had caused them to chunk their knowledge so they could access it easily.

Ray Kroc had visited so many restaurants as a Multimixer salesman that he could quickly analyze what the McDonalds brothers had going for them.

Louis Pasteur had spent 11 years studying fermentation before he tied it together in his mind with exposure to air.

And King Gillette had spent his entire business life working with people who sold disposable items to the public.

Obviously it's not realistic to suggest that you can develop intuition by first spending a decade or more becoming an expert in the area of your problem. However, you can simulate that condition by soaking your mind with information about the problem.

➡ Key points from this chapter

▶ We handle more than seven points by "chunking" information.

▶ What many people think of as intuition is really thinking fast by chunking underlying knowledge.

▶ So-called intuition comes from experts soaking their mind with information about the problem.

Chapter 22

Improving Intuition With Right-Brained Thinking

In Chapter 20, I taught you that people who have a golden gut—the divine gift of intuition—think faster by chunking information. They're experts in their field and know how to chunk large segments of information. This enables you to improve your access to short-term memory and to long-term memory, which increases your ability to concentrate.

In problem solving you usually don't have the luxury of being an expert in the area in which you're dealing. However, you can simulate that condition by saturating the mind with facts about the situation.

In this chapter, I'll teach you how to position the mind for intuitive thought by shutting down the left brain and stimulating the right.

How your brain works

Both sides of the brain gather in the same information, but make decisions differently. The left brain codes the information in verbal form and uses logic to make decisions. The right brain absorbs the information emotionally and makes decisions intuitively. We're still learning and speculating about how all this affects our behavior.

Some researchers wonder if what Sigmund Freud called the subconscious is really just the non-dominant side of the brain. In this country, 85 percent of us favor the left brain, the logical side. That means your left brain dominates your conscious thought. What Freud called the subconscious, may just be the influence of the right brain. It may just be coincidence, but Freud was one of those very rare people who couldn't tell his left hand from his right. I don't mean that facetiously. In his book, *The Origins of Psychoanalysis*, he said, "To make sure which was my right hand, I would quickly make a few writing movements."

Left-brain dominance also may explain "déjà vu," that sudden feeling that you've been there before. It may just be one side of the brain transmitting an image a split second ahead of the other side.

Dr. Benjamin Libet, a psychologist with the University of San Francisco, points out the brain starts to seek information about 4/10ths of a second before we're aware of it. That isn't speculation; he proved it in scientific tests. Four tenths of a second is a significant amount of time, which in itself may explain intuition. The right brain starts working on a problem 4/10ths of a second before the logical left brain becomes aware of it. Sometimes the right brain will come up with the correct answer a split second before the left brain realizes it.

The right brain gets drunk first. When the right brain is aroused, it impedes the judgment of the left, causing slurred speech and impaired problem solving.

The right brain goes to sleep first and wakes up last. That explains why you have those wonderfully creative ideas as you drop off to sleep. When you wake up in the morning, your left brain is screaming, "How could you have ever thought a dumb idea like that would work?"

The right brain shuts down under stress; it has a very delicate tilt mechanism. The left-brained engineer can plow through adversity without any problem. She says, "Oh, so the shuttle blew up when we launched it? That's interesting. Well, we'll keep working at it until we get it right."

The right-brained playwright will be so upset over one bad review that he'll go drive a cab for a year.

The creative mind shutting down under pressure causes many problems in problem solving. Very often stress and problem solving go hand in hand. Just when you need your creative right brain the most, it shuts down and leaves town. The ability to control the left and right sides of your brain when making decisions is a key skill leading to good problem solving.

Left Brain	Right Brain
4/10 of a second slower to start working on a problem.	Faster to start working on a problem.
Goes to sleep last.	Wakes up last.
Wakes up first.	Gets drunk first.
Handles stress well.	Shuts down under stress.
Likes to solve problems analytically.	Likes to solve problems intuitively.
Makes decisions slowly.	Makes decisions quickly.

Whether you're predominantly left or right brained makes a big difference in the way you solve problems.

Left-brained people like to solve problems with an organized approach. They do research, list and analyze possible solutions, and assign possibilities to the possible options. They like to research if anyone has faced the problem before, and if so, go with proven solutions.

Right-brained people like to solve problems by getting a feel for what works and finding out how other people feel about it. This is the "throw it up against the wall, run it up the flag pole" brigade. They may find out that somebody else has faced the same problem before, but they're just as likely to pick a different solution—just to see what happens.

▸ Key points from this chapter

- ▸ Both sides of the brain gather in the same information, but make decisions differently.
- ▸ The left brain codes the information in verbal form and uses logic to make decisions.
- ▸ The right brain absorbs the information emotionally and makes decisions intuitively.
- ▸ The right brain shuts down under stress.
- ▸ The ability to control the left and right sides of your brain when making decisions is a key skill leading to good problem solving.
- ▸ Left-brained people like to solve problems with an organized approach.
- ▸ Right-brained people like to solve problems by getting a feel for what works and finding out how other people feel about it.

A problem difficult at night is resolved in the morning after the committee of sleep has worked on it.

—John Steinbeck

Chapter 23

Controlling the Left and Right Sides of the Brain

Your ability to be intuitive depends on the degree of access you have to the deepest levels of your mind. You prepare your mind for intuition by forcing your logical left brain to shut down, and letting your creative right brain dominate. By shutting down the left brain, and letting the creative right brain take over, you prepare your mind for intuition.

Strangely enough, you can do that in two diverse ways: by either stimulating your brain waves, or relaxing them. In a high state of arousal, your right brain dominates and you become more creative. This is what happens at football games, sales rallies, and cheerleading sessions. Jogging and other forms of exercise also keep you in a high state of arousal, because the improved blood circulation pumps glycogen to your brain, and glycogen is rich in energy.

The opposite is also true. In a low state of arousal, the right brain also dominates. A boring assembly line task shuts down the left brain and causes daydreaming. This is how hypnotists put you under. They freeze the left brain with the boredom of a pendulum or metronome, talking to you in a monotone voice, and then implanting suggestions in the right brain.

Attorneys use much the same procedure in court by making witnesses answer question after question for two or three days. Their left brain effectually goes into a coma, which causes the right brain to take over and they emotionally blurt out something they had no intention of revealing.

Some seminars are designed to bore you

I once attended a four-day seminar that exploited this phenomenon of shutting down the right brain. We sat in a hotel ballroom listening to a trainer drone on. We'd submitted ourselves to a very controlled environment, unable to do anything outside the very rigid rules they'd set up. We weren't even allowed to go to the bathroom. We couldn't challenge the viewpoint of the trainer. They designed all this to numb our ability to be creative. We submitted to this because of the constant assurance that on the fourth day we'd "get it." What we eventually got was a heavy dose of B.F. Skinner for the masses. They told us not to worry about life, because we were so strongly conditioned by our experiences, that we'd always react the way we'd been programmed to react, regardless of what we tried to do. Their advice was to relax, and let life happen to us.

The audience greeted this astounding assertion with cheers of delight and left the room thrilled with their $400 investment. All I got out of it was a sore behind.

You can experience a shift from left-brain to right-brain thinking in many little instances in your life once you're aware of the phenomena. For example, analyze how you decide what to do the next time a homeless person asks you for a handout. If I have to walk through a poorer area of a city, I put some dollar bills into a separate pocket. If a needy person approaches me, I can be generous without having to bring out my wallet. Once I was in downtown Chicago and saw a shabbily dressed man approaching me for a handout. My right brain was reaching into my pocket for a dollar bill, when he asked me if I could spare a quarter. My logical left brain immediately took over. I thought, "What on earth can you do with a quarter?" Because, as any salesperson will tell you, a confused mind says no, I moved on without giving him the dollar.

Reacting to a request for a handout is only one of many instances where you can experience your mind shifting from one side of the brain to the other. Once you become aware of this syndrome, you'll find yourself experiencing it all the time.

Boredom and repetition arrest the left brain and let the right brain dominate.

What arrests the right brain, and why would you want to do that?

If you're in a fearful situation it's very good to know how to shut down the right brain, which loves to exaggerate danger. Let the left brain take over for a while. My son Dwight once talked me into doing a bungee jump. This was the craze in California at the time that involved going to a high place, tying elastic cords to your ankles, and diving off.

The bungee rope is 100 feet long, but it has a huge amount of stretch in it. It's the kind of rope the military uses when they parachute helicopters into a battle zone. You free fall 100 feet and then the stretch in the rope takes you another 100 feet—almost to the ground. Then you bounce back up in the air and down again and up again. Upon reflection, that makes as much sense to me as leapfrogging a unicorn, but there I was, standing on the platform, which was so far up in the air that the people down below looked like ants. The wind was whistling past me and fear was clutching my heart with a vise-like grip. I was beginning to think that the best thing that could have happened to me was to have crashed my car on the way there, and have broken both my legs.

If they'd have asked me to stand on the platform, and said to me, "Just go ahead and jump whenever you feel like it," I'd still be standing there. I could feel my right-brain imagination taking over. I was imagining the rope breaking or being too long, and seeing myself smashing into the ground below.

To shut off that creative right brain, all the other jumpers gather around on the ground way below. They're peering up at you and yelling, "Five! Four! Three! Two! One!" That left-brain concentration on counting momentarily shuts down the right brain. Instead of imagining all the things that might happen, you're now concentrating on what you have to do.

On the count of "one" you reach your hands above your head, bend your knees, and launch yourself off into space. Suddenly you're free falling, and the ground is hurtling toward you at 60 miles per hour. Just when you're convinced that something has gone horribly wrong, and you're going to smash into the ground, your fall is magically arrested. It's like committing suicide and having God snatch you back at the last moment! For a brief second, you hang there, neither going down nor up. Then the stretch in the rope wins the tug of war with gravity, and you hurtle back into the sky again. During the ascent you experience what only a handful of astronauts have experienced in the past: complete weightlessness. You're aware that you're going up, but the tug of the rope and the tug of gravity is so evenly balanced that you feel as though you're floating. Suddenly you're at the top of your float upward, and panic overcomes you again, as you start back down. Three or four times you bounce up and down, until the stretch in the rope is exhausted.

The countdown from the other jumpers has a magical effect. It shuts down the right side of the brain, and lets the left side take charge. The logical left side of the brain isn't creative enough to conjure up all the horrible things that might happen to you, and you jump. Believe me, it's the only thing that could pry you off that platform!

Emotion sells but is sometimes a hindrance

Typically, salespeople are in the business of stimulating right-brain thinking because emotion is what sells. But sometimes it's necessary to do the reverse. For example, real estate agents often take a listing where the owners have a tremendous amount of emotional involvement with the home, because they've lived there for years. Unfortunately for the salesperson, the buyer isn't going to have that emotional attachment to the house. The real estate agent must arrest the owners' right-brain thinking and bring them back to the logical world. They start by calling it a house not a home. In real estate terminology, people buy a home but sell a house.

With a little practice you'll find that you're quickly able to control which side of the brain dominates your thinking. When you can do that at will, you're close to being able to create intuitive flashes of inspiration.

➡ Key points from this chapter:

▶ You can learn to develop your intuition if you know how to access the deep levels of your brain.

▶ The key is to shut down the logical left brain, and let the creative right brain take over.

▶ You can do that in two ways: either by stimulating your brain waves or by relaxing them.

▶ Practice shutting down the left brain by boring it with repetitive tasks or thinking.

▶ Practice stimulating the right brain with excitement and activity.

Chapter 24
Moving Away From the Problem

Here's the next step to intuitive thinking: moving away from the problem, either physically or mentally. By doing this, you more clearly focus your concentration on the problem. Some impressive thinkers have seen the value of mentally moving away from the problem.

Thomas Edison was famous for the catnaps that he took during the day, saying they gave power to his thinking. He faced the biggest challenge of his life when a fire destroyed his movie and record producing plant. It was the only moneymaking venture he had at the time, and the profits from it were needed to support his laboratory. According to his son Charles, as soon as the fire was under control, he announced that he was rebuilding. Almost as an afterthought he added, "Oh, by the way. Anybody know where we can get some money?" When nobody had an answer, he took off his coat, rolled it up to make a pillow, and fell asleep at the table.

Also, many great flashes of intuition have been attributed to physically moving away from the problem.

John Moran, the founder of Hycel Corporation, worked for months on a design for an automatic blood analyzer. He finally gave up, and left on vacation. He woke up at a resort hotel the next day, and he could see the right design in his mind. He hastily sketched it out, flew home, and built the prototype. When he sold the company to a German conglomerate 14 years later, they paid him $40 million.

Getting away, particularly to a foreign country, removes any preconceived parameters you've put on the problem. When you're in your working environment, you're surrounded by invisible chains of what's done or not done in your industry.

Just as people will do things in the tropics they'd never dream of doing at home, so the inhibitions of the mind are removed in a foreign land. One of the smartest business decisions I ever made came to me when I was sitting on a beach in Tahiti, looking out over the peaceful waters to the magical island of Bora Bora. Often an idea has popped into my mind as I've absentmindedly browsed through a street market in Peru or Ecuador. Physically removing yourself from the problem-solving arena reduces your anxiety level, and helps you stay calm and self-assured. Also it re-energizes a mind that may be drooping from mental fatigue.

Of course you don't have to fly to Tahiti to get away from the problem. You can mentally get away from the problem by just closing your office door and having your calls held.

The length of time away from a problem may be microscopic. I'm sure you've had the experience of trying desperately to recall a name. It wasn't until you stopped thinking about it that the name came into mind.

Okay, so you're in the middle of solving a big problem. How do you know if you should keep on pressing for a solution? Perhaps you need to move away from the problem and say what Beethoven would say when inspiration wouldn't come to him: "Nothing comes to me today; we shall try another time."

It's time to move away from the problem when the same solution keeps recurring but it doesn't seem to be the perfect answer. You need to distance yourself from the problem when you're having trouble concentrating, or feeling frustrated, or you can't focus clearly on the problem.

An alarm should go off—it's time to clear the building when irritability sets in, when you see physical signs of stress or fatigue, or when you're having trouble articulating what you're thinking. These are all signs that tell you to take a break.

Once you've moved yourself away from the problem, whether it's to a beach in Tahiti, or simply into your office with the door closed, you need to induce intuitive thought. It's time to develop inner calm, because at the very center of inner calm is mental clarity.

To do this, try this exercise: Close your eyes and roll your eyeballs up slightly, until you feel the slight pressure of them touching the optic nerve. Stay perfectly still and start thinking of the muscles in the toes of your right foot. Let your muscles go limp, like a handful of rubber bands. Do the same thing with your left foot. Gradually work your way up through your legs, mentally relaxing each muscle. Let this wave of calm relaxation work its way up through your body, until your shoulder and neck muscles start to go limp. Then move it up into your brain, until your thoughts stop dancing around and you're at perfect peace.

The objective of this mini meditation is to reduce mental noise and create a lowered state of arousal. A lowered state of arousal shuts down the left brain and stimulates the right. *Mental noise* is a term psychologists use to describe thoughts and images that come to you solely from your memory. They interfere with intuition because any thought that comes from memory carries with it preconceived views.

It's a fascinating contradiction: Generating intuition is hard work. Yet the harder you work, the less you generate intuition. Intuition happens when you work hard at moving your mind away from work. "I've never heard of a completely out of the blue insight," says Dr. Perkins of Harvard University, author of *The Mind's Best Work*.

Intuition reflects your ability to make connections between completely separate pieces of information stored in the brain.

As I told you in Chapter 20, an expert does it by chunking information together, so his or her mind can better juggle the complexities of the problem. You can do it by learning how to subdue the left brain and letting the right brain go to work for you. Lowering mental noise induces intuition and helps you make those connections better and faster. Good problem solving requires you to perfect your left-brain ability to sift details, and to blend it with right-brain creativity. Finally you return to left-brain logic to verify your hunches.

▶ Key points from this chapter

▶ It's important to get away from the problem, either mentally, or physically.

▶ Mentally can mean the brief relaxation exercise that I taught you, or taking a quick nap.

▶ Physically can mean closing your office door and having your calls held, or leaving the country.

▶ Moving away from the problem liberates your mind to be creative.

Chapter 25

Finding New Answers With Creative Thinking

If you find yourself at your desk with your head in your hands agonizing over a problem, I can make one very basic assumption: There are additional options of which you're not yet aware. Somewhere out there is the answer you're looking for, but you haven't found it yet.

Finding that missing answer is where creative thinking comes into play. In this chapter I want to take you through a series of steps that will help you create additional options. Even if you've already come up with a good answer to your problem, even a seemingly perfect answer to your problem, you should still go through these steps. Once the pressure is off to find an acceptable solution, you release creative thinking powers and often come up with an even better idea. There's magic in the second solution.

Experts in creative thinking talk about vertical and lateral thinking. Vertical thinking is the traditional way, building on one thought at a time as you move to a conclusion.

Lateral thinking doesn't require that kind of foundation of thought. It attempts to trigger great leaps in thinking by the brain. With this new way of thinking you can jump to a solution without taking all the steps between. I'll show you how to do this by taking you through a 10-step checklist of right-brain creative thinking ideas.

We might think of the 10 creative thinking steps as disciplined daydreaming. Like me, you've probably been conditioned against daydreaming by criticism from teachers and parents. It's considered cruel and unusual punishment in this country, but schoolteachers in England can throw a piece of chalk clear across a room. They could hit a daydreaming student on the head with the accuracy of a Patriot missile.

An efficiency expert once told Henry Ford he should fire one of his executives. He told Ford, "Every time I go by his office, he's just sitting there with his feet on his desk. He's wasting your money."

Ford replied, "That man once had an idea that saved us millions of dollars. At the time, I believe his feet were planted right where they are now."

Unfortunately, we live in an age where we glorify machines that think, but condemn people who try to. For effective creative thinking, we need to learn the art of disciplined daydreaming. Shutting down the left brain and letting the right brain dominate, the way I showed you in Chapter 23, prepares your mind. The next step is to go through the following 10 steps to creative thinking. Here are the 10 right-brain ways to expand your options:

Step one: Visualize the opposite of the situation

The first creative thinking way to expand your options is to visualize the opposite of the situation. There are many ways to do that.

The first is to reverse the objective. A distributing warehouse company in New England did this with great success. I learned about it when I trained their buyers to negotiate better. They were in a situation where the warehouse workers weren't filling the orders fast enough. The obvious solution was to put in more supervision, so they'd get a better job done by the workers. Instead they reversed the objective and considered no supervision at all. Then what would it take to make it happen? Well, it would take incentives for the workers. It would take a system of teams, where each team member policed the action of other team members, because they were competing for the choice of work schedules, and other perks. The company decided to take a chance on it. It was the best move they ever made. The money they were previously paying for supervisors could now be allocated to worker incentives. Both production and morale went up.

Let's look at another situation where reversing the objective may be effective. Los Angeles, where I live, has a horrendous traffic problem. The average daily commute increased to 53 minutes according to census bureau director Louis Kincannon. By the time you've found a parking space that's two hours a day you're wasting. Caltrans, which is the state agency that handles highways, sees car-pooling as the answer to the problem. They think all we have to do is cram half a dozen people in every car and all our problems will go away.

Spend half an hour on an L.A. freeway during rush hour and you will know that's not right. Fully 95 percent of the cars have only one person in them. To drive in the car pool lane, you only need to have a second person in your car. Of the 5 percent doing that only a small percentage of them actually set up a stranger with whom to ride, meaning that the car pool lane didn't change their commuting habits at all. Car pool lanes get used so little that they are now allowing hybrid cars to use them to reward them for using cleaner air cars.

What if we reversed the objective to see how few people we could get into a car? Well, we could have smaller cars. What's smaller than a car? A motorcycle. If everybody rode a motorcycle to work, we could make traffic lanes half the size. Overnight we could double the capacity of our freeways, to say nothing of solving our fuel crisis and pollution problem. Well, that's too extreme, but we could add motorcycle lanes to the shoulder of the freeway right now. But motorcycles are unsafe. Why can't we develop a safe motorcycle? One with a protective bubble around it for weather and safety?

The winner of the 2010 Automotive X-Prize Alternative Class $2.5 million prize was the Peraves E-Tracer. It's a motorcycle completely enclosed in Kevlar fiberglass. It's an electric plug-in vehicle that is a hybrid. It can go 200 miles on a gallon of gas and hit a top speed of 200 miles per hour. It's twice as long as a normal motorcycle and inside are two bucket seats. It's too expensive right now but if they can get the volume up and the cost down it would solve all our traffic problems.

See how reversing the objective can stimulate creative solutions?

Let's say that the solution you're working on right now has the objective of increasing profits as quickly as possible. What if you reversed that objective and thought of it as being to lose money as quickly as possible? How would you go about that? By uncovering the ways you lose money, perhaps you'll discover where your profit is slipping through the cracks.

You're familiar with how FedEx got started, of course. Fred Smith wanted to start a business that would move envelopes and packages from one place to another overnight. Everybody knows the fastest way between two points is a straight line. Try reversing that objective. Visualize the opposite of a straight line. To him, it was the notion of shipping everything first to his hometown of Memphis and then shipping it back out. From this came Federal Express.

The problem of noise has baffled scientists for years. Ever increasing levels of noise have become a plague on our modern society. All their attempts to do something about it centered on baffling the noise, to reduce the sound waves that reach us. Then somebody tried visualizing the opposite of that. What if, instead of reducing the noise sound waves, we increased them?

It didn't seem to make any sense, but they tried it anyway. What they discovered was very intriguing. If you exactly duplicate a noise, the two sets of sound waves cancel each other out, and the human ear can't hear either one.

Scientists created a device that would listen to the noise, digitalize the sound, and re-create it. Remarkably, it works well: The two sounds cancel each other out, and what you hear is silence. It lead to the noise-cancelling headsets that so many frequent flyers wear. I wouldn't be without my Bose headphones. I always used to wonder why flying coast-to-coast was so tiring. You're just sitting there with nothing to do. What's so exhausting about that? The answer is that noise pollution is exhausting you. With noise-cancelling headphones you arrive perky and raring to go. Now they are developing devices that will fit on car mufflers, lawn mowers, leaf blowers, and other sources of noise, and will silence them. Isn't that something?

Another form of reversing the objective is contrarian thinking. When everybody in your industry is thinking one way, start looking in the opposite direction. The Gillette Razor Company knew that 60 percent of razors sold were the "10 for a dollar" disposable kind. Instead of introducing even cheaper razors, they introduced the Sensor Razor. It sells for 25 percent more than the existing best-selling razor, and it's a huge success. They now sell a Fusion Power Razor that lists for $28.99.

Always question conventional wisdom. Why is everybody thinking this way? What would happen if they were all wrong?

Step two: Examine the environment

Creative thinking step number two is to examine the environment in which the problem exists, not the problem itself.

When President Reagan got to the White House, he found he'd inherited a world gone mad. Ironically, mad is an acronym for the insanity I'm talking about: MAD (Mutually Assured Destruction). Since the Soviet Union first developed Intercontinental Ballistic Missiles (ICBMs) we'd relied on this policy to save the world from destruction. The policy said that if you attack us, we'll have a big enough second strike capability to destroy you in return. Through the years, each side kept increasing their arsenal of nuclear warheads to maintain balance. By 1981, the superpowers were looking like two people standing at opposite ends of a swimming pool filled with gasoline. Each of them with a stockpile of cigarette lighters, threatening to ignite the gasoline and destroy them both.

Edi Amin, then-president of Uganda, once seriously proposed that the United Nations ban all conventional weapons in favor of low-priced hydrogen bombs distributed equally around the world!

Instead of looking at the problem, President Reagan looked at the environment in which the problem existed. He realized it existed only because the Soviet Union could afford to continue the buildup. What would cause them to say, "We can't do this anymore"? The brilliant strategy he came up with was Star Wars, which would be a missile defense system that would shoot down any incoming missiles well before they reached their target.

We'll probably never know whether Star Wars was the biggest bluff of all time, but it worked. The Soviets said they couldn't afford to stay in this game, and folded their hand. Most scientists doubt that Star Wars was ever feasible, but the research did produce the Patriot missile air defense system that was so effective in the Iraqi war.

This idea of looking at the environment, rather than the problem, is invaluable in raising children. If you have three or more children, chances are you have one that's giving you fits. Instead of worrying yourself sick about them, start examining the environment in which they exist. With whom do they hang around? What books are they reading? What movies are they watching? Who are they texting? What Websites are they going to? That's where you'll find the answer to your problem.

Step three: Visualize yourself finding the perfect answer

Creative thinking step number three is to visualize yourself finding the perfect answer. Visualization may seem old hat to you, but there's no denying its power. "You become what you think about," said my hero, Earl Nightingale.

Jack Nicklaus said this about visualization: "I never hit a shot without having a very sharp, in focus, picture of it in my head. It's like a color movie. First I see the ball where I want it to finish, nice and white and sitting up high on the bright green grass. Then the scene changes quickly and I see the ball going there. Its path, trajectory, and shape—even its behavior on landing."

Visualization really does work. However, in a stressful problem-solving situation, we tend to picture negative results. Instead of visualizing the favorable results of a good decision, we become obsessed with the penalties of a bad decision.

I think it's very revealing that there are 43 words in the English language that describe a mistake: aberration, error, blooper, blunder, boner, boo-boo, bull, bungle, confusion, delusion, flaw, flub, fluff, fault, gaffe, illusion, inaccuracy, inadvertence, lapse, miscalculation, misapprehension, misconception, misinterpretation, misjudgment, misprint, misstatement, misunderstanding, miscue, misstep, mix-up, muddle, neglect, omission, underestimation, overestimation, oversight, rock, slight, slip, slipup, snafu, trip, and faux pas. But there isn't a single word that describes the opposite of a mistake, the act of doing something right. With such a focus on negativity, it's no wonder we have trouble solving problems!

I find visualization especially helpful in dealing with people. I use it if I'm going into a meeting where I think people will raise objections to my proposal. Instead of worrying myself sick about the conflict, I shut my office door, close my eyes, and visualize their warm response to my proposal. It has a magical effect on people. I don't know why it works, but I can get to New

York without understanding how a plane works. I just know that when you push thoughts of love and encouragement out into the world, they don't dissipate, they circulate. The power of visualizing a warm response to your proposal is an awesome force.

Step four: Imagine all the assumptions you've made are wrong

The fourth creative thinking step is to imagine that all the assumptions you've made about the decision are wrong.

What if all the expected opposition to your plan fell away? You're nervous about introducing a price increase. What if your customers said, "That's great. We were wondering why you didn't do it a long time ago?"

That buyer may be thinking, "Are you charging us enough to make a good profit? You're the best supplier of this product in the industry. If you went out of business, we'd be in serious trouble."

Every salesperson assumes that buyers want to pay less. I challenge that in my sales training classes. I think that there's one thing Americans love to do and that's spend money. We do it better than anyone else on the planet! And the only thing better than spending your own money is to spend your company's money. Those buyers want to pay more, but you have to do two things: You have to show them why they should spend more, and you have to convince them that they couldn't get a better deal however hard they tried.

I was in Hong Kong recently to promote my books, which are being published in China in Simplified Chinese. There was a line around the block waiting to get into the Louis Vuitton store. They had to hire guards to control the people who wanted to get in to spend $3,000 for a purse. Now tell me that people want low prices!

My friend Henry Hoche turned his Victorian style mansion, the Innisfree in Glenville, North Carolina, into a beautiful bed and breakfast inn. He assumed I'd still want to come and stay with him free. Not so, I'd rather pay and know he would welcome me again.

Take, for example, a company that increases its staff, but now doesn't have enough parking spaces. They assume they have a problem because everyone wants to park close to their work. Let's imagine for a moment that the assumption they made is wrong. Instead of people wanting to park close, they really want to park as far from work as possible. That sounds crazy, but thinking like that makes you realize that people don't want to drive to work at all. They'd love it if you'd send a limousine for them. From this thought, the idea of vanpooling was born.

This exercise of imagining your assumptions are wrong moves you away from the obvious solutions to your problems, and generates more options.

Step five: What if you knew you couldn't fail?

The fifth creative thinking step is to imagine what you'd do if you knew you couldn't fail. If you could work miracles, what would you do to solve the problem? When I was young and knew everything, I thought it was self-defeating to set unrealistic goals. If you weighed 300 pounds, you shouldn't dream of becoming a racehorse jockey. Now I'm not so sure. That kind of thinking didn't get blind climber Eric Weihenmayer to the top of Mount Everest.

The *what if* line of thinking is absolutely fascinating. What if we didn't have to ship things, but we could transport thcm by beaming them up as Scotty does in *Star Trek*? Perhaps it was just such a thought that inspired Amazon to create the Kindle book-reading machine and Apple to produce the iPad that together are revolutionizing book distribution.

What if children didn't have to learn everything their parents knew? What if we could genetically implant a brain cell that would transmit all knowledge to them?

It was this kind of *what if* thinking that caused Albert Einstein to discover the theory of relativity. He said, "What if I could travel from point A to point B faster than the speed of light? The people at point B could clearly see I was with them. On the other hand, they could look back to point A and see I was still there. Because my image was only traveling at the speed of light, it would appear I'd be at point B, before I'd left point A." From Einstein's *what if* thought about the speed of light came the whole theory of relativity and also his whole theory that time isn't a sequential thing. That all time is happening at one instant. We've just translated it into a sequential thing so we can better comprehend it.

You don't have to be an Einstein to have the *what if* theory make a big difference in your life. I always used to feel that I was limited by what I could afford to do. For example, I'd drive into a town and make a decision on a hotel based on what I could afford to pay. Then one day I was driving into Geneva from Paris. Geneva's one of the most expensive cities in the world, so I knew the price of a hotel room would be outrageous. I started thinking where I would want to stay if money was no object. Ah, yes, this beautiful luxury hotel next to the lake, in a corner suite with two balconies. What if I knew I couldn't fail to negotiate the price with the desk clerk? First you select the hotel and then you figure out how you can afford to pay for it. As luck would have it, the desk clerk was from England. We struck up a conversation, and he gave me just the room I wanted at a bargain price.

From then on I quit limiting my vacations to what I felt I could afford to pay. Instead I started thinking, "Where in the world would I like to go, and what would I like to do when I got there?" Having decided that, then I'd figure out how I was going to pay for it. That may seem like a little change in thinking to you, but it will make an amazing change in your lifestyle.

In problem solving, we all too often limit our thinking to preconceived parameters. Don't exclude any possibilities until you've decided what you'd like to accomplish if you could work miracles.

Step six: Run the decision by a series of role models

The sixth creative thinking step is to run the decision by a series of role models.

The role models don't have to know they're your role models. In the speaking industry I have several people I admire greatly and whenever I'm faced with a decision, I run it by them. I don't call them, and they never know. I just bounce it off them in my mind. It's amazing how often I've stopped myself from making a stupid mistake because I knew my role models would tell me to forget it.

It's also amazing how often creative solutions have opened up to me because of running it by a role model. For example, a couple of times I've faced what appeared to be an impossible travel schedule. I'm booked to speak at a large convention in Maui, and I have an opportunity to earn a large speaking fee talking to another group in Orlando the next day. But I call the travel agent and she tells me it's impossible; it can't be done. The last flight that would connect to Orlando, leaves Maui at 2:00 p.m., so there's no way.

In my mind, I run it by one of my role models. This is my line of thought: "Well, my role model wouldn't have a problem with this, because he could afford to rent a private jet to fly him there. Well, I can't afford to do that, but have I checked the possibility there may be a corporate jet with an empty seat? Could I get as far as Los Angeles on a commercial flight and then rent a corporate jet and still have it pay off for me? Perhaps the company in Orlando has a jet that's flying in from the West Coast that could take me. Another thought that might come into my mind is that my role model wouldn't have a problem with this, because he'd have enough clout to move the date of one of the speaking engagements. I haven't approached the companies on this possibility, but maybe I should talk to them about it."

In your business, you might be faced with a major financial problem and you say to yourself, "Okay, my role model is Ben Bernanke, chairman of the Federal Reserve Board. What would Ben Bernanke do?" You think, "Well, that's ridiculous. Ben Bernanke wouldn't have a problem with this. He could pick up the phone and talk to a dozen people who could restructure debt for him, and resolve the problem." And that triggers the thought, "Well, why couldn't I do that?" or "Who could I contact that could do it for me?"

Perhaps you have a security problem at your plant in Nebraska. Your role model for this kind of problem is the director of the FBI in Washington. The moment you run it by your role model in your mind you think, "Well, sure, he wouldn't have a problem with that. He'd simply pick up the phone and call the Attorney General of the state of Nebraska and things would start to move." Then you think, "Well, wait a minute, why can't I pick up the phone and call the Attorney General's office? I may not get to talk to him or her, but I'd get to talk to somebody there."

Tom Monaghan, who turned a $500 investment into a $480 million fortune with Domino's Pizza, had Ray Kroc, the founder of McDonalds, as his silent role model. He didn't get to meet Kroc until he was already a huge success, selling more than $200 million a year. Ray Kroc said, "I'm gonna give you some advice. You've got it made now. You can do anything you want, make all the money you can possibly spend. Slow down, take it easy. Open a few stores every year, but be very careful. Don't make any new deals that could get you into trouble. Play it safe."

Finally Monaghan blurted out, "But Mr. Kroc, that wouldn't be any fun!"

Kroc jumped up from behind his desk and pumped his hand. With a big grin, he said, "That's just what I hoped you'd say!"

Step seven: Visualize the opposite of the situation

Creative thinking step number seven is thinking backward. With this one, you imagine the desired solution, and you start working back and visualizing how it all came together. It's a great way of forcing the subconscious mind into play.

This is a terrific way to identify the missing link in the problem. What's the one thing that's creating the problem? What's the one thing that would solve the problem?

Many years ago, when I was a retail store merchandise manager, we had a shoplifting problem. Experienced shoplifters knew how to approach a rack of clothes near the door, and swoop up a great armful of them and then be out of the door before we even realized what was happening. They'd jump into a waiting van and drive off before we even had a chance to get a license number or a description of the crooks. We could seal off the doors but we wanted to run a store that was customer friendly. We identified the missing link as the short amount of response time we had for this occurrence. Then we started to think, "How could we slow them down?" The solution came to us that we'd simply alternate the direction of the hangers on the rack. When the shoplifters tried to swoop up an armful of clothes, they wouldn't come off together.

Step eight: Look at the problem from another planet

Creative thinking step number eight is to look at the problem from another planet. Sometimes we're so close to a problem, we get so stressed out that we can't see the issues clearly. Canadian advertising genius Marshall McLuhan is famous for saying that we don't know who discovered water, but we know it wasn't a fish, because fish are too immersed in it to see it clearly. I would respond that we don't know who discovered stress, but we know it wasn't a corporate executive because corporate executives are swimming in it all the time.

On the wall in my office I have a large poster that's a very graphic painting of the planets. There's a huge ball of the sun on one side and then stretching off into the distance are Mercury, Venus, then Earth, the little blue and white one. Then, Mars, Jupiter, Saturn, Uranus, Neptune, and poor little discredited Pluto. Pointing down at the little blue and white planet Earth is one of those directional markers that says, *You Are Here*. Just to put things in perspective for me!

When I'm faced with a problem, I like to take myself away in my mind to one of my favorite places. In my mind, I ride the train up to the top of Victoria Peak overlooking Hong Kong harbor. Not the modern new railway but the rickety old one that existed when I first went there in 1960. I go to the *Peak Cafe* at the top, have a cup of tea and look out over the view. As a young man I first fell in love there, and the sweet memory still lingers. In the distance I can see what used to be the sleepy little fishing village of Aberdeen, way back then. Now it's a mass of high rises. We walked there through the hills, so many years ago, my new love and I. At a waterfall, she stopped to play with some butterflies, and I showed off by climbing the fall. I slipped and cut my head, and rushed back down to her, blood pouring from the wound, but more concerned that she'd forgive me for being so stupid. We hurried down the trail to Aberdeen to get the wound stitched up. Without thinking my hand goes to the small scar on my forehead that still lingers 50 years later. My mental journey takes me across an ocean, and more importantly, back through a few decades. It helps me to put my problems into perspective, even though it's only a trip I'm taking in my mind.

Step nine: De-focus the problem

Creative thinking step number nine is to de-focus the problem. Don't be too focused on what you want to come out of this. It's just as important to defocus the decision, as it is to focus on it.

Mary Kay Ash never intended to create a cosmetics company. She was working in catalog sales and started to write a book to help women like herself, who were being under utilized in business. Her idea was to help other women over-come the obstacles she encountered. Yet, she didn't know how to write a book—so she started listing the things in business that held women back. Then she listed the positive things that did help women succeed. Without realizing it, she had written the marketing plan for Mary Kay Cosmetics. The business that intuitively popped into her mind avoided all the traps, and of-fered all the opportunities. From this, she built an $800 million a year industry. Had she stayed focused on writing the book, it never would've happened. Oh yes, she did eventually write the book, and it did become a best-seller: *Mary Kay on People Management*.

Fred Smith really started Federal Express as a courier for Federal Bank Documents, which is where it got its name. When that didn't work out he was flexible enough to use the same business plan to start an incredibly successful package moving business.

Step ten: Look at the problem with childlike innocence

Creative thinking step 10 is to look at the problem with the innocence of a child. Remember the movie *Big*, in which Tom Hanks was mystically given a grown up body and then got a job as an executive at a toy company? Although he knew nothing about toy manufacturing, he was very effective as a creative executive. Why? Because he could cut through the corporate clutter to get to the essence of the problem. They may have based that movie on an actual incident, where a consultant convinced Mattel Toy Corporation to put children on their board of directors.

Look at your problem as if it was being explained to you for the first time. Think about how you'd react.

For example, you may be faced with an inventory shrinkage problem at one of your factories. Your natural tendency might be to bite the bullet and hire detectives to increase the amount of security guards at the plant to decrease the employee theft.

A child might ask, "How much do all those security guards cost you? How much are the employees stealing?" It could well be that security is costing you more than the goods they're stealing.

Then a child might say, "Why don't you do away with all those security guards and just trust the employees?"

As an experienced executive, this may be a laughable example to you, but your innocent side may say, "Perhaps that would work. Perhaps if we trusted the employees more, they'd steal less."

In fact, I know of a company that did exactly that. Faced with a problem of employee theft, they eliminated the cost of their security guards, which was more than the amount they were stealing. Then they told the employees they trusted them; and in the future they expected them to police each other, so nobody let the team down. To their surprise and delight, employee theft dropped off to almost nothing and the reduced cost of security jump-started their bottom line.

I want to let a real expert have the last word on creative thinking. He was probably the most creative thinker of his century. Walt Disney once said to a young visitor to Disneyland, "If you'll remember four words, you'll grow up to be a very wise man. The first word is: think. Think about the values and the principles that guide you. The second word is: believe. Believe in yourself based on the values and principles that guide you. The third word is: dream. Dream about something that you want to do and then do it based on your belief in yourself about the thinking that you have done, about your values and principles. The last word is: dare. Dare to make your dream become a reality because of your belief in yourself, because of the thinking you've done, about the values and the principles by which you are going to live. Son, just in case you forgot, those four words are think, believe, dream and dare."

I think with those four words, Walt Disney gave us the framework with which to solve any problem:

- ❯ Think through the problem, so you thoroughly understand it.
- ❯ Believe that you can find the perfect answer.
- ❯ Dream of a creative solution.
- ❯ Dare to follow through and make it happen.

❯ Key points from this chapter

In this chapter we've focused on 10 creative thinking ways to expand our choices in solving the problem. That's called divergent thinking—expanding the possibilities.

- ▶ Visualize the opposite of the situation.
- ▶ Examine the environment in which the problem exists, not the problem itself.
- ▶ Visualize yourself finding the perfect answer.
- ▶ Imagine all the assumptions you've made about the decision are wrong.
- ▶ Imagine what you'd do if you knew you couldn't fail.
- ▶ Run the decision by a series of role models.
- ▶ Imagine the desired solution and start working back, visualizing how it all came together.
- ▶ Look at the problem from another planct.
- ▶ Don't be too focused on what you want to come out of the decision.
- ▶ Look at the problem with the innocence of a child.

Section Five

Logical Problem Solving

*Don't bother people for help without first trying
to solve the problem yourself.*

—Colin Powell

Intuitive decision-making does seem like a wonderful answer to all our problems—if we can make it work. If it always worked, all we'd have to do is sit back, do a few exercises to shut down the left side of our brain, and put all our wonderful one hundred billion brain neurons to work on the problem. Don't ask me who counted them. That's a big number. If you counted one a second it would take you 3,171 years to do it, according to Professor Eric Chudler of the Washington University. While we're at it he also says that the theory that we only use 10 percent of our brain neurons is a myth. We use all of our brain cells.

Nobel prize winner Dr. David Hubel tells us there are one hundred trillion links between those cells, give or take a few trillion. The corpus callosum, the connecting link between the two halves of the brain, contains about 200 million fibers. It can transmit two billion pieces of information per second. And all that gray matter is sitting up there doing nothing more challenging than watching Vanna White on *Wheel of Fortune*! Let's drop into an alpha state, and have them go to work. Then at any moment the perfect solution will pop into our minds, and we can start yelling "Eureka."

There's a big problem with that line of thinking: Intuitive thinking won't work on some decisions. The intuitive mind can't handle some pretty basic stuff. Some things, you just have to sweat out with logic.

Let me prove that to you, by having you consider this mental exercise:

> I live in La Habra Heights, which is just outside Los Angeles. Let's say that one morning I decide to drive up the scenic coast road to San Francisco. I'm going to visit my youngest son, John, when he attended Menlo College. It's a 400-mile drive, and will take me all day. It's a fun drive, through San Luis Obispo, past Hearst Castle, through Big Sur and Monterey. I start at eight o'clock and because I'm driving slowly, admiring the scenery, it takes me 11 hours. Two days later, I start driving back, again leaving at eight in the morning, following the same route. However, this time I'm in a hurry and drive much faster, reaching home in eight hours.
>
> Here's the question: Will I be at any point on that road, at exactly the same time of day, as I was there two days before?
>
> Put the book down, and think about it for a while.

Okay, what was your conclusion? Probably you said no; it isn't possible that I was at the same point at exactly the same time of day. I did the southern part of the journey in the morning when I was going north. I did the southern part of the journey in the afternoon when I was coming south. If I were driving at exactly the same speed, there'd be a point in the middle that I'd pass at exactly the same time. But I wasn't driving at the same speed. So the answer has to be no.

Uh, uh, uh! The answer is yes; there is a place where I would be at the same point at the same time of day, on both trips. This is an example of intuitive problem solving telling us the wrong answer. It takes logical problem solving to find the right answer.

Now let's use logic on the same question, and see how obvious it really is. Instead of one driver making a round trip, think of two drivers making the trip on the same day. I leave Los Angeles at eight in the morning, and my son John leaves his college in San Francisco at eight the same day. He drives much faster than I. Isn't it obvious there'll be a point in the journey when we'll pass each other? And when we do, aren't we in the same place at the same time?

Here's another example. Cognitive scientist Peter Wason came up with a very interesting experiment. He displayed four cards that looked like this:

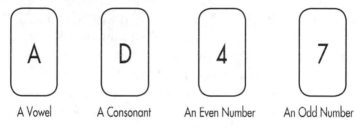

| A | D | 4 | 7 |
| A Vowel | A Consonant | An Even Number | An Odd Number |

Note that there was one vowel, one consonant, one even number, and one odd number. Then he came up with a question about these cards, which asked, "Which two cards do you have to turn over to prove that if a card has a vowel on one side, it has an even number on the other side?"

Put down the book and see if you can figure it out.

Only 4 percent of the people he tested got it right. Obviously, you turn the A over to be sure it has an even number on the other side. But most people select the 4 as the other card; to be sure it has a vowel on the other side. And that's the wrong answer! The right answer is the 7; to be sure it doesn't have a vowel on the other side.

The interesting thing about that is, not only did 96 percent of the people get it wrong, but it's almost impossible to understand why you should turn the 7 over, and not the 4.

Just as in the Los Angeles to San Francisco problem, our intuitive mind lets us down.

Here's another example. You are a contestant on a television quiz show. You are told to pick one of three doors to win the prize behind the door. One door has behind it a car; the other two doors have goats.

Let's say you pick door number one. The host opens door number three to reveal a goat and asks you if you want to switch your answer from door one to door two.

Your conclusion is that it doesn't help to switch. You have a 50 percent chance of winning the car, whichever door you pick.

But that's the wrong answer. If you switch to door two your chances of winning go from 33 percent to 66 percent. Say what? That's ridiculous! There are two doors and one car. The answer has to be that your chance of winning is 50/50 regardless of which door you open. But that's wrong.

When *Parade Magazine* columnist Marilyn vos Savant ran this puzzle in her column she got 10,000 letters (including 1,000 signed by PhDs) telling her that she was wrong, that the chances are 50/50.

You may remember the movie *21* where Kevin Spacey, playing a Harvard mathematics professor, presented the same problem to his students.

As amazing as it seems, the answer is that you do increase your chances of winning a car from 33 percent to 66 percent by switching your choice. If you don't believe me Google or Bing it and follow the discourse of math professors who still don't accept that that is the right answer.

Math professors can have a field day explaining this to you with very complicated formulas. Let me attempt a very simple explanation. If you switch doors you have been able to pick two of the three doors, giving you a 67 percent chance of winning. If you don't switch doors you have only chosen one door of the three, which gives you a 33 percent chance.

The point here is that some problems can't be solved with intuition, however good at it you become. You simply need logic, and that's what we're going to talk about in this section.

Chapter 26
Go or No-Go Decisions

Good problem solvers know that intuition alone won't solve our problems, however good at it we get. In this chapter I'm going to teach you ways to statistically evaluate the choices you have. You won't want to use them all, of course. Use the one with which you feel most comfortable, depending on the seriousness of the problem with which you're faced. The bigger the problem, the more involved the procedure you'll want to select.

Having determined that you do indeed have to choose between different alternatives, the process becomes more involved. Now you must match the problem to a problem-solving method. In this chapter, I'll cover a situation when the decision is a choice between go and no-go.

- ▶ Should you go skiing at Lake Tahoe with your friend, or should you stay home and finish remodeling the den?

- ▶ Should you accept that job offer, or shouldn't you?

- ▶ Should you buy out your competitor, or not?

There are three ways to solve a go or no-go problem: the Coin Toss, Check Listing, and Quantified Evaluation.

Method one: The Coin Toss

Let's start with the simplest method: the Coin Toss.

Hey, don't laugh, this is serious stuff. There's a lot more you can do with a coin than start a football match. My son Dwight taught me this while we were on a tour of Central America. For many years, I've had this ambition of driving down from my home in Los Angeles to Buenos Aires, Argentina, but I could never find the six months or so it would take to do it, so I decided to take a month and do a test run to Central America and see what it would be like.

Dwight and I drove all the way from my home in Southern California, through Mexico and Guatemala into Honduras. One night we were in Tegucigalpa, the capital of Honduras, and our problem was that we couldn't decide whether to go on down to Managua, Nicaragua, or swing back through San Salvador and head across Guatemala to Belize. We talked it over for a couple of hours over dinner, and still couldn't decide. Neither of us felt strongly enough about it to push for one side of the decision, or the other.

My son said to me, "Let's toss a coin."

I told him, "Come on, Dwight! I don't want to decide something as important as this, based on a coin toss. There's a civil war going on in El Salvador. What if we go there and get shot? How's that going to look in my obituary, when it comes out I decided to go there based on a coin toss?"

He told me, "There's more to it than that, Dad. We toss the coin, and then decide."

"Give me that again. Have I spent 26 years raising a complete imbecile?"

"Trust me, Dad. You'll love it. You'll be talking about it in your seminars one day."

We tossed the coin. Heads we go to Nicaragua, tails we go to El Salvador. It came up heads—Nicaragua. Dwight said, "Now, how do you feel about it?"

It was amazing. A moment ago, I simply couldn't decide. Now I was clearly disappointed it hadn't come up tails. I really wanted to go to El Salvador and Belize. It sounds stupid, but it's an amazingly effective way to make up your mind. We went into El Salvador, didn't get shot, and then had some of the best adventures of our trip in the remote eastern side of Guatemala, putting the four-wheel drive to the test on the worst roads I've seen anywhere in the world, staying on a remote ranch where the owner had just been executed by the military, and exploring ancient Mayan ruins with a new Israeli friend.

Try the Coin Toss when you're having trouble making up your mind.

Let's say you own a car dealership. There's a Chrysler dealership down the street that's having tough times, and it's up for sale. You've done all the analysis and it's still a toss-up in your mind. The deal isn't so great that you'd be crazy to turn it down, but on the other hand it looks like a pretty good opportunity. Close your office door, so your employees won't think you've cracked up, and toss a coin. Now how do you feel about it? Is your mind fighting the decision? Are you thinking, "I really didn't want to take on that much extra work"? Or is it thinking, "Now I know it's the right thing to do"?

If you use this frequently, you may find you don't even have to get as far as tossing the coin. Most people tend to think of heads as positive, and tails as negative. Very often you pick heads for the one you subconsciously want to do. You say to yourself, "Heads I'll buy it, tails I won't." See if a pattern develops. If you're pleased when it comes up heads, and disappointed when it comes up tails, you don't even have to toss the coin to know which way to decide!

Remember that this method doesn't provide a creative answer to your problem. It just tells you what your gut feels about the problem.

Method two: Check Listing

Another effective way to solve a go or no-go problem is Check Listing.

This is similar to a mission control countdown, or a pilot's checklist. Your list is made up of items that must be on a go status in order for you to proceed.

For example, the problem you face may be to hire or not hire a particular person for a position in data processing at the bank you run. You list minimum requirements for that position, which might include:

1. Must have five years experience in data processing, of which at least one year must be in banking.

2. Must be willing to relocate downtown later, if that becomes necessary.

3. Shouldn't be taking a cut in pay to come work for us. (People who take a cut in pay are frequently dissatisfied, and move on quickly.)

4. Must be able to pass a physical exam.

CHECK LISTING		
Go	No-Go	Requirements
✓		Must have five years experience in banking
✓		Must be willing to relocate downtown later
✓		No cut in pay to join us
	?	Passes physical exam
Decision: Acceptable for employment subject to passing physical exam.		

You might give this checklist to your human affairs director (or whatever it is you call your personnel director these days) to establish parameters for the position. Or you may use it yourself—to evaluate the choices they bring to you.

With Check Listing, you go down the checklist to be sure the applicant qualifies in each of the areas, or you put this person on a no-go status until this requirement is waived or deleted.

Method three: Quantified Evaluation

A more complicated way to solve a go or no-go problem is what I call Quantified Evaluation.

You make two separate lists: one listing those factors that favor making a decision, and the other lists the factors against making the decision. Now you rate each factor on a scale of 1 to 10.

I used Quantified Evaluation to decide where I should write this book. I have a second home in the mountains at Lake Arrowhead, about an hour and a half's drive from my home. Part of me was saying I'd be better off writing up there, and part of me was saying I'd be better off at home. First I listed the reasons for going to the lake. I

QUANTIFIED EVALUATION			
IN FAVOR		OPPOSED	
8	FEWER INTERRUPTIONS	8	REFERENCE BOOKS
6	CREATIVE ENVIRONMENT	6	PUBLIC LIBRARY
5	RELAXING ATMOSPHERE	4	LESS LONELY
		9	AVOID BACK AND FORTH TRAVEL
19	DIVIDED BY 3 FACTORS = 6.3	27	DIVIDED BY 4 FACTORS = 6.8

thought of three reasons: fewer interruptions, a more creative environment, and a more relaxing atmosphere.

Then I thought of four reasons for writing at home:

1. I'd have all the reference books from my home library.

2. At home I have access to high-speed Internet.

3. I'd be less lonely at home.

4. I wouldn't waste time making several trips up and down the hill, to fly to speaking engagements and to take care of regular business.

The next step is to rate each of these factors on a scale of 1 to 10. Remember that in this system, all the ratings are positive. Five and below isn't a negative; it's just less of a positive.

In favor of going to Lake Arrowhead, I rated the factors this way:

Fewer interruptions:	8
Creative environment:	6
Relaxing atmosphere:	5
Total	19

Next I divided the total of 19 by the three factors, and came up with a score of 6.3 in favor of going to the lake.

In favor of staying home, I rated the factors this way:

Access to my home library:	6
Access to high-speed Internet:	8
Being less lonely:	4
Time saved:	9
Total	27

This total score was 27, divided by four factors, for a score of 6.8.

Because the score in favor of staying home was 6.8 and the score for going to the lake was 6.3, I stayed home. I hope you agree I made the right choice!

Remember that with Quantified Evaluation, there are no negatives. You rate only the positive factors and then average them.

I've given you three ways to make a decision when the choice is between doing something and not doing something. In the next chapter I'll show you how to make a decision when you have to choose between two different possibilities.

➠ Key points from this chapter

▸ There are three ways to make a go or no-go decision: the Coin Toss, Check Listing, and Quantified Evaluation.

▸ The Coin Toss helps you understand what choice your subconscious mind would make.

▸ Sometime you don't have to toss the coin. Which did you choose to be heads?

▸ Check Listing focuses on the minimum requirements for success.

▸ Quantified Evaluation makes you break down the different elements involved and rate them against your two choices.

> *No problem can be solved until it is reduced to some simple form. The changing of a vague difficulty into a specific, concrete form is a very essential element in thinking.*
>
> —J.P. Morgan

Chapter 27

Choosing Between Two Ways to Solve a Problem

In this chapter, we'll move to a more complicated level of problem solving: when you have to make a choice between two dichotomous possibilities. A dichotomy means that you only have two solutions available to you, and they are contradictory or mutually exclusive. Remember that a true dichotomy is rare. If you use the creative thinking checklist I gave you in Chapter 25, you can usually come up with more than two choices. However, if you have narrowed it down to only two choices, there are three ways of making the decision.

Method one for dichotomies: The 1 to 10 rating system

Rating everything on a scale of 1 to 10 makes problem solving easy. Once you've assigned ratings, the choice is obvious. The advantage is, it forces you to evaluate the choices systematically.

> You can't decide whether to open your next frozen yogurt store in Tulsa or Oklahoma City. Your file on each location is 3 inches thick. It seems as though the more information you get, the harder the choice becomes. Try the 1 to 10 test. How do you feel about Tulsa? About an 8. How do you feel about Oklahoma City? About an 8.5. Why do you feel that way? You don't know, but those 100 billion brain cells have been working on it, and that's what they're telling you.

Don't use this to override good, solid information. But if you simply can't decide, it's a good way to break a mental deadlock.

The 1 through 10 rating system is also a terrific way to extract information from other people. You're a salesperson and you can't get a fix on whether your customers are ready to place the order or not. Ask them, "Where are you on this—on a scale of 1 to 10? Ten meaning you're ready to order right now, and one meaning you wouldn't take it if we gave it to you." I've never had anyone refuse to give me a number.

They might say, "Well, I guess I'm at a 6."

And you say, "Help me out. What would it take to get you to a 10?"

They might respond, "I'll tell you what's bothering me. I see your figures about the projected savings, but I need something stronger than that. For me to go with this, I'd have to be guaranteed that kind of savings."

Bingo! In a few short seconds you've isolated the objection, and almost got the buyer's commitment to buy if you can satisfy his or her one concern.

Or you might be trying to hire a key executive for your company. You need to find out if the money you're offering is going to be enough to get him or her on board. Ask, "How do you feel about coming with us? On a scale of 1 to 10? Ten meaning you're ready to decide right now, and one meaning you've already ruled it out?" You'll get an instant fix on how this person feels, without having to come right out and ask if you're offering enough money.

It's one of the most powerful tools I've ever learned for finding out what's going on in a person's mind, and it seems to work every time.

I'd been using the 1 to 10 rating system for decades before I became aware of a very significant thing. Not everybody's scale goes from 1 to 10.

I have three children: Julia, Dwight, and John. One winter we rented a condominium in Park City, Utah, for a ski vacation together. One evening we were discussing whether, for a change, we should drive around the mountain and ski Snowbird. We couldn't seem to decide. I asked John, the youngest one, "On a scale of 1 to 10, how do you feel about going to Snowbird?"

He said, "I'm at a 7." This wasn't particularly helpful to me. Then he said something very insightful. He said, "But remember on my scale, I don't have an 8, 9, or 10."

That's true: John is very low-key. He never gets particularly excited about anything, but on the other hand, he never gets depressed either. The summer that we spent mountain climbing in Europe he reached the top of the Matterhorn—an incredible accomplishment, considering he'd only climbed two mountains before, and this was his first rock climb. I met him at the 14,000-foot level and threw my arms around him, with tears in my eyes. I said, "I can't believe you made it!"

He said, "Wasn't that what I was supposed to do?" In effect, he doesn't have an 8, 9, or a 10 on his scale, nor does he have a 1, 2, or 3. His range goes from 4 to 7. On the other hand, Dwight, my older son, has a scale that only includes 1, 2, 3; 8, 9, and 10. He either loves something, or hates it.

Be aware of this. You may not have an 8, 9, or 10. For you, a 7 may mean "run with it!"

Method two for dichotomies: The Ben Franklin

More involved than the 1 through 10 rating scale is the Ben Franklin approach.

In a letter to British chemist Joseph Priestley, Franklin explained his system this way:

> "My way is to divide a sheet of paper into two columns; writing over the one Pro, and over the other Con. Then, during the three or four days consideration, I put down under the different heads short hints of the different motives, that at different times occur to me, for or against the measure. When I have thus got

them all together in one view,
I endeavor to estimate their
respective weights; and where I
find two, on each side, that seem
equal, I strike them both out. If I
find a reason pro equal to some
two reasons con, I strike out all
three. If I judge some two reasons
con, equal to some three reasons
pro, I strike out the five; and thus
proceeding I find at length where
the balance lies; and if, after a day
or two of further considerations,
nothing new that is of importance
occurs on either side, I come to a
determination accordingly."

| The Ben Franklin Approach ||
Pros	Cons
1.	1.
2.	2.
3.	3.
4.	4.
5.	5.
6.	6.
7.	7.
8.	8.
9.	9.
10.	10.

He called it moral, or prudential algebra. It works well when the choice is between doing something or not doing it. It's not very effective for multiple choices.

Salespeople find the Ben Franklin approach very helpful in convincing buyers. On one side of the sheet they list all the reasons for going ahead with the decision. On the other they list the reasons for not going ahead. Of course they're very helpful in coming up with reasons for going ahead, and a lot less helpful in thinking of the negatives.

Method three for dichotomies: The report card method

The third method of deciding between two options, is the report card method.

Al Neuharth, the newspaper genius who later started *USA Today,* used this method when he was trying to decide whether to move from Knight Newspapers in Detroit, to Gannett. He was doing well with Knight Newspapers, and the decision didn't seem as obvious as it appears in hindsight. He listed the 10 things that were most important to him, personally and professionally, and rated them on a scale of 1 to 10. A major point was that Gannett was a publicly traded company, which he could eventually control. Knight was family owned, so he could never have complete autonomy. He gave Knight Newspapers a 10-point "loyalty" bonus. Even so, Gannett won 94 to 92. Close, but enough to change the face of newspaper publishing in this country, because at Gannett he expanded the company to where it owned small newspapers all over the country. It became the only company with enough printing plants that *USA Today* could be composed centrally and printed locally.

Let me explain the report card method, by telling you how I used it to decide which vehicle to buy for our trip to Central America.

My son Dwight, who was taking the trip with me, wanted a Nissan Pathfinder. This is the rugged four-wheel drive that looks like a four-wheel drive should—a real man's vehicle. He had the dealer bring one to the house for me to test-drive, and it impressed me. The other option we'd narrowed it down to was a four-wheel drive Ford Aerostar, which is a minivan.

We listed the factors that were important to us, and then rated them. First was gas mileage, which was very important because we'd be driving so far. We gave the Ford an 8, and the Nissan a 5. Remember that on a scale of one to 10, a 5.5 is neutral. This means that 5 or less is a negative, and 6 or more is a positive. If you think of 5 as neutral, you skew the scale with an optimism factor.

Availability of parts in Central America was significant, and had caused us to rule out many other possibilities. We gave Ford an 8 and Nissan a 6. Although we never spent a night in the vehicle, we thought it might be a factor, and gave Ford an 8, and the much smaller Nissan a 2. For comfort, we gave the Ford an 8 and the Nissan a 6. Then we considered how useful the vehicle would be to me after the trip. Here the minivan was a big advantage over the smaller Nissan, 9 to 5. It also got a big plus for carrying space, 8 to 4. The van was $8,000 cheaper than the Nissan,

Factors	Nissan	Ford
Gas Mileage	5	8
Availability of Parts	6	8
Sleeping In Vehicle	2	8
Comfort	6	8
Useful After Trip	5	9
Carrying Space	4	8
Low Price	6	8
Off Road Handling	9	7
Dependability	8	6
Desire	9	5
Total	60	75

so low priced that it got an 8 compared to a 6. For off-road capability, the Nissan was clearly the winner, 9 to 7. For dependability, we considered the fact the Ford was using a brand-new electronic four-wheel drive. As it turned out, it behaved beautifully, but we had our doubts. We gave the Ford a 6 and the Nissan an 8.

Finally we rated each on a lust factor. How badly did we want to own them? Here the Nissan won overwhelmingly! It got a 9. The poor old minivan only got a 5.

Then we added the scores up. The Ford Aerostar got a 75 rating, compared to the Nissan's 60, so we went with the Ford, and didn't regret it. It worked well, even in Eastern Guatemala, on the worst roads I've seen anywhere in the world.

The report card method obviously has flaws, the biggest one being it doesn't give weight to the various factors. But it worked for Al Neuharth, and it served us well also.

➡ Key points from this chapter

In this chapter, I've taught you three ways to solve a problem when you have two alternatives from which to choose:

▶ The 1 to 10 rating system.

▶ The Ben Franklin approach.

▶ The report card method.

In the next chapter, we'll move on to more complicated possibilities.

Chapter 28
Handicapping Critical Decisions

Now let's move from dichotomies to more complicated problems. If you have more than two choices, problem solving becomes more involved. In this chapter, I'll cover how to decide between three or more possibilities, when the outcome of each choice is predictable.

There's a very efficient system to handle this, which I call Handicapping:

First: Consider your objective only in *positive* terms. What are you trying to accomplish? Don't focus on what you dislike; consider only the positive aspects of each option.

Let's say you're thinking of making a career change. Negative concerns might be:

➧ I hate my boss.

➧ I'm starving to death on what they pay me.

➧ I feel trapped.

➧ I hate the weather in Buffalo.

Dwelling on the negatives like that doesn't induce creative thought. Instead it stifles it. You should consider only positive objectives, which might be:

> ⚫ I want to move to a larger company that could offer greater opportunity.

> ⚫ I want to earn more money.

> ⚫ I'd like to live in a warmer climate.

> ⚫ I want a better benefits program.

> ⚫ I want a greater challenge.

> ⚫ A different boss might see me in a more favorable light.

> ⚫ If I move, I could improve my position within the company.

> ⚫ I could get a better title.

Next, on a scale of 1 to 10, consider how you feel about each of these factors? For example, you might give a low rating to money and title. Your major concern might be opportunity and the chance to end up running the company. (If you're younger than 30 years old, I hope that is the way you're thinking. Don't worry about the money when you're young. Be more concerned about how you will learn and grow on the job.) The importance you give to each of these is a personal thing, but let's say that you rate them on a scale of 1 to 10, like this:

		IMPORTANCE
1.	Greater opportunity.	10
2.	More money.	8
3.	Better location.	6
4.	Improved benefits.	6
5.	Greater challenge.	9
6.	Better boss.	8
7.	Improved position.	7
8.	Better title.	4

Next, put your creative mind to work and list all the available alternatives. This might be a list of the companies in your industry meeting your criteria.

Evaluate each company against your list of criteria weights. Give them a rating on a scale of 1 to 10 as you feel about them in each of those elements. Now multiply the weight factor by the rating number. For example, opportunity was a weight factor of 10 for you, and you give this company a 7 for that. Ten times 7 is 70, so that's the score this company gets in that element. Benefits got a weight factor of 6, and you give this company a 7 for its benefit package. So they get 6 times 7, or 42 points for this. Here's how your chart might look then:

	IMPORTANCE	x LIKELIHOOD	= SCORE
1. Greater opportunity.	10	7	70
2. More money.	8	8	64
3. Better location.	6	8	48
4. Improved benefits.	6	7	42
5. Greater challenge.	9	6	54
6. Better boss.	8	7	56
7. Improved position.	7	8	56
8. Better title.	4	8	32
TOTAL SCORE FOR THIS COMPANY			422

In that way, you rank each company. This might give you a list of 20 different companies that might have what you're looking for, rated by how closely they meet your objectives.

Make a tentative decision on the best alternative, based on the total scores of each company. Then examine that alternative for any possible adverse consequences. Perhaps there's something you overlooked. Perhaps you didn't think of football when you made your list, but when you contemplate a move to Amarillo, you suddenly realize how much you're going to miss pro football.

List alternative actions that you'd take in the event the decision doesn't go as you expect. What if none of the 20 companies on your list want to hire you? What if you move to Houston and can't stand the weather? What are you going to do then?

You may feel that this is getting to be too complicated to be worthwhile. Remember, however, that you won't be using a Handicap Table to decide where to go to lunch. You'll only be using it for life-changing decisions like a career move, or buying a home. It is well worth taking the time when you're involved in critical decisions like that.

Handicapping works well as long as there isn't much uncertainty involved. And in the case of changing jobs, there isn't much. You'll apply for work with all 20 and compare the offers that you get.

➼ **Key points from this chapter**

▶ Consider the problem only in positive terms, not negative terms.

▶ Take your list and rank them in terms of how important they are to you on a scale of 1 to 10.

▶ For each element multiply the importance by the rank that you gave to each choice.

▶ Add up the total scores for each item on your list of positives.

▶ Handicapping is much more accurate than the Report Card method because it ranks every consideration.

Section Six

Gathering Information

I learned that Singapore was defenseless.
I did not know. I was not told.
I should have asked.

—Winston Churchill

The key to solving a problem is to get the right information, so let's talk about becoming an expert at gathering information. If you hired me to come and solve your problem for you, what's the first thing I would do? Right! Ask you a bunch of questions. Think how much money you'll save if you've answered all those questions before I start charging you for my time.

English author Rudyard Kipling laid out the framework for this process in his poem "I Keep Six Honest Serving Men."

I keep six honest serving-men

(They taught me all I knew);

Their names are What and Why and When

And How and Where and Who.

Note that What, Why, When, How, Where, and Who are all open-ended questions, which means questions that cannot be answered with a yes or no. Open-ended questions, as any salesperson will tell you, are much better at gathering information.

First consider how much information should you gather? In business, gathering information is very expensive. You hire an advertising agency to take surveys and do test marketing. You quickly learn you can spend millions of dollars and still not learn very much. You must balance the cost of gathering information with the necessity of having the right information.

Still, it's really hard to solve a problem when you don't have enough information. Maybe you'll be lucky, but chances are you won't. Anytime you're faced with a problem, you should be saying to yourself, "Do I have enough information to make a wise decision?" If you do, then you should go ahead and start working on solutions to the problem. If you don't, then you're better off calling a time out, until you get the information you need.

The other point to consider when gathering information is: Under how much time pressure are you? If time is a big consideration, it may limit the amount of information you can gather. When you're trying to solve a problem about marketing a new product, you must balance the need for information with the danger of delaying the decision too long. By waiting too long to make the decision you may let the competition get the jump on you.

The best tip I can give you on gathering information is to have a system in place that gathers the kind of information that could be useful to you one day. Don't wait until you need to know, to start finding the information. For example, if you're going to buy a new car within the next year, watch for car reviews when you're checking your computer for e-mail and updated news, and copy and file reviews of cars that may interest you. You don't even have to read the reviews; just accumulate them. Clip dealer ads from the classifieds so you build data on pricing. Then when you get ready to make the decision, you'll already have all the information you need right at your fingertips.

On my computer I have a huge file of bits and pieces that I've accumulated over the years. They are saved in dozens of files by topic. It's a tip that I picked up from a preacher whose challenge was writing and delivering 50 sermons a year. Then if I decide to write a chapter for this book on happiness, for example, I'll be able to pull up my happiness file and soak up information about all the studies that have been done and the opinion pieces that have been written over the last 10 years. Couldn't I just do a Google or Bing search when the time comes? I suppose so but that would be like trying to take a sip from a fire hose. I prefer knowing that I've saved what I thought were the best tips on the topic.

Perhaps you have an idea that someday you'd like to open a restaurant. Maybe it's something vague and far in the future you're considering, but start accumulating information right now. Every time you see an article about a restaurant, clip it out and just file it away. When the time eventually comes that you want to make a decision, you'll have a wealth of information to help you solve problems and make wise decisions.

Chapter 29

Gathering Information Is the Key to Good Problem Solving

Even industrial giants can be victims of poor information

Even the most sophisticated of companies can be a victim of poor information. The chairman of Ford Motor Company, Don Petersen, was about to conclude a brilliant career. Due to retire, he made a final major decision to buy Jaguar Motors for $2.5 billion. They paid five times book value for a company that sold only 50,000 cars a year. BMW and Mercedes sell 10 times as many. At the time, Jaguar had a serious quality problem. J.D. Powers showed their problems per car as 100 times greater than their competition. The Jaguar X-Type was rated by *Time* magazine as the sixth-worst-quality car of the decade.

Petersen really didn't have to pay J.D. Powers much money to find that out. He could have called me and I would have told him free of charge. My XJS, which is their 12-cylinder model, was an absolute disaster. When it ran, it was one of the finest cars on the road, but most of the time it was in the shop. Finally, the engine blew up and they wanted $11,000 to put a new engine in the car!

After Ford had bought Jaguar, they sent a team over to inspect the factory. They found out why the quality was so bad. Reports came back that it was probably the worst car plant in the world. That's really saying something when you think of Yugos and Trablants. *Time* magazine called the 1975 Trablant "The automobile that gave communism a bad name." Ford spent another $10 billion modernizing the Jaguar plant. According to *USA Today*, Ford dumped both Jaguar and Land Rover in 2008, selling them to Tata, an Indian company better known for its trucks and cheap passenger cars. Ford had paid $5.3 billion for the two companies. Tata paid only $1.7 billion. If a large successful company like Ford can fall victim to poor information, it's clear that we need to be especially cautious.

Beware of gathering too much information

Like the ingredients for a recipe, information has to be the right stuff in just the right quantity.

Don't fall into the trap of gathering information for the sake of doing it. Henry Ford once proudly pointed to one of his cars and said, "There are exactly 4,721 parts in that model." The visitor was amazed that Ford would know something like this. Later he asked an engineer if the number was accurate. The engineer said, "I don't know and even if it is, I can't think of a more useless piece of information."

As you'll see later, gathering too much information can actually prevent you from solving a problem. Your objective isn't to accumulate information; it's to gain knowledge. We gather information by getting the right answers from other people or sources. We gain knowledge from asking ourselves the right questions. Jonas Salk, the discoverer of the polio vaccine, said, "Discovery is a quest. You perceive it by questing." By which he meant, keep on asking the questions.

How important is gathering information?

We can probably agree that information can give you power, particularly if you have information that the person creating your problem does not have. Also, the more information you have, the less likely you are to make a bad decision. Being good at gathering information is important because the more you know, the better your intuition will be. Let me explain why.

Remember when you're new at something you have to concentrate on every detail? Such as your first day driving a car? You had to make all those separate decisions: putting the turn signal on, shifting down, taking your foot off the gas pedal, and putting your left foot on the clutch and your right foot on the brake. All the little details were individual things you had to do. Then as you became more familiar with it, those things came to you automatically. In a fluid motion you could go through them, without having to think about them.

The more information you have, the more you have a framework within which to solve problems well. Instead of consciously having to think through every step, your intuition can be turned loose as it flows through the problem.

The Japanese spend a lot of time on this. American businesspeople who do business in Japan will tell you that it's very hard to figure out how Japanese people make decisions or solve problems. They simply want to keep on asking questions until the optimum course of action becomes obvious.

▶ Key points from this chapter

▶ In business, information gathering can be expensive. Determine the minimum amount you need to be well informed.

▶ How much time pressure are you under? Don't let the need to gather more information cause you to miss an opportunity.

▶ Try to generate information before you need it. Create a research file on your computer and drop everything of interest into it.

▶ Even industrial giants can be victims of poor information. Think of Ford's purchase of Jaguar.

▶ Beware of gathering too much information.

Chapter 30

Information Drift

As you gather information, understand that human beings are very imprecise in the way we gather and analyze information. I call this Information Drift.

Think of a ship that's leaving San Francisco harbor sailing out under the Golden Gate Bridge. Its destination is Hong Kong, and the navigator has laid out a course of action and knows the route to take. He's probably already adjusted for ocean currents, prevailing winds, and other such things. However, as they proceed on this four- or five-week journey, many things will cause the ship to drift off course. Winds, tides, currents, and moon phases will all come to bear on it, and for each of those factors, the captain of the ship has to compensate.

It's the same way with gathering information. As we gather information about the decision, we need to recognize that many things cause us to drift off course. If we don't realize it, we'll make a decision with inaccurate information. There are seven major ways that our gathering of accurate information can drift off course. As you gather information to help you solve the problem, you need to run through a checklist:

✓ Are you proceeding based on information that was just the easiest to obtain?

> That's Availability Drift.

✓ Are you biased in analyzing this information because of your background?

> That's Experience Drift.

✓ Are you rejecting certain information because it conflicts with your existing prejudices?

> That's Conflict Drift.

✓ Are you working on information of particular interest to you?

> That's Selectivity Drift.

✓ Are you guilty of anchoring to a particular figure?

> That's Anchoring Drift.

✓ Are you giving additional emphasis to information just because something has happened to you recently?

> That's Recency Drift.

✓ Are you guilty of favoring information that supports your own beliefs?

> That's Favorability Drift.

The more we're aware of the tendency to drift when gathering information to solve a problem, the more likely we are to gather accurate information. Let's look at each of these in more depth.

Availability Drift

Availability Drift refers to our tendency to give more weight to information that's more readily available to us. In simple language, the more we're aware of something, the more we tend to give it emphasis it doesn't deserve. News coverage is often the cause of the Availability Drift, because newspapers and television news shows don't give equal emphasis to events.

Let me ask you four questions to convince you of this:

1. Are you more likely to get colon cancer or die in an automobile accident?

    You probably said automobile accidents, because we hear more about automobile accidents than we do people getting colon cancer. In fact, more than twice as many people get colon cancer than die in automobile accidents. The American Cancer Society predicts 102,900 deaths from colon cancer in the United States. The National Highway Traffic Safety Administration reports only 42,000 deaths from automobile accidents.

2. Do more people die of murder or pneumonia?

    You may well say murder, because we hear more about it. In fact, three times as many people die of pneumonia. Expect around 52,700 people in the United States to die of pneumonia; 16,000 will be murdered.

3. Is the suicide rate higher in New York or New Mexico?

    New York has the lowest suicide rate in the nation, about one third the rate of states like New Mexico and Arizona, which you'd think would be much less stressful. If you said New York, you were also a victim of Information Drift in a different way: New York is really a very rural state. Because we hear so much more about their urban areas, we tend to think of all New Yorkers living in big cities.

4. Do more people die in shooting accidents, or by drowning?

    Three times as many people die by drowning than in shooting accidents. About 5,000 people drown, and only 1,400 die in shooting accidents.

Experience Drift

The second type of Information Drift is Experience Drift, which refers to our tendency to see things in terms of our personal or professional interest. As pool hustler Johnny Irish once said, "How about that guy? Can't even run six balls and he's president of the United States!" A bowler might say, "He bowls a gutter bowl and still gets elected president!"

If you were asked to guess if more people attend basketball games or baseball games, you'd probably pick your favorite sport. You'd have trouble believing that auto racing is really the most highly attended spectator sport in the world. According to *The London Times*, more than 258,000 people attend one event alone: the Grand Prix at Le Mans.

If you were born in America, you'll have trouble believing that the most widely viewed sporting event in the world is a soccer match. More than 700 million people watched the final of the World Cup from South Africa in 2010.

Now you can see how Experience Drift causes us to get off course. An example of this is the CEO in an automobile company who has come up through the luxury car division. The competition jumps into the minivan business but he passes it off as a fad that won't last just because of his background.

It's easy to see it in others; it's much harder to see it in ourselves. We understand that a president who was a civil rights lawyer in Chicago is going to view poverty in a far different light than a president who is the son of a president and the grandson of a Senator. But can you see the areas where your experience has colored your world?

Conflict Drift

The third type of drift is Conflict Drift. We tend to reject information that conflicts with our beliefs. For example, if we think watching television is a waste of time, we have trouble believing the average American watches 153 hours of television a month (according to Nielsen). That does not include programs watched on computers, cell phones, and iPads. Vegetarians have trouble believing the average American consumes more than their weight in flesh every year.

When something conflicts with our beliefs, we tend to reject it, to disbelieve it. As a young man, I started a career with Montgomery Ward, the department store chain, and was given many lectures about watching for shoplifters. Because I would never steal anything, I dismissed it as somewhat paranoid. One day, I was standing on the balcony of the store, watching an attractive young lady in the fabric department. She suddenly reached out, took a zipper from the rack and put it in her purse. I stood there, having trouble believing what I knew I'd just seen. She must have sensed that I was watching her, and quickly put the item back in the rack. Because state law said that she must leave the store (at very least the department) before I could detain her and call the police, I could do nothing about it.

It explains why so many people are able to embezzle money from their employer, and get away with it for years. The first time I caught a trusted employee embezzling many thousands of dollars from me, I was so stunned that I couldn't believe the clear evidence in front of me. It's hard to read about embezzlement without a comment from their supervisor that they couldn't believe "this nice person would do such a thing."

Be sure that you're not rejecting information simply because it conflicts with your beliefs.

Selectivity Drift

The fourth reason for inaccurately analyzing the information is Selectivity Drift. We can't absorb everything, so we screen out what doesn't interest us. Let's say you run a sporting goods manufacturing company. You're an avid golfer but have little interest in bowling. Your natural tendency is to be keenly aware of things affecting the golf division, and be oblivious to what's going on at the bowling ball factory. You need to compensate for that.

Casual observation of things is called soft input by researchers, as opposed to scientific observation, which is hard input. Good problem solvers learn to verify soft information with hard information. Let's say you're an executive at General Foods. You go down to your local supermarket to pick up some groceries. It seems as though everybody has a can of Folgers's coffee in his or her grocery cart. That's a Smuckers product. Before you jump to conclusions that you have a problem with Maxwell House sales in the area, you check the hard data on your computer.

In business, Selectivity Drift can be very expensive, as you can see in this story about Howard Hughes. After World War II, he became involved in sophisticated weapons making. He had hired two very talented young scientists, Dr. Simon Ramo and Dr. Dean Woolridge, who were former classmates at the California Institute of Technology. Ramo had gone to General Electric, and Woolridge had gone to Bell Telephone Laboratories, before they began working together again at Hughes Aircraft. Their venture into military electronics went very well indeed. However, it didn't particularly interest Howard Hughes, who was spending more time in Las Vegas courting actress Terry Moore than he was at Hughes Aircraft headquarters in Culver City. Friction broke out among the management, and they all appealed to Howard Hughes to re-solve the problem. Because it didn't interest him as much as his other ventures, he let it slide. It was a disastrous move.

Ramo and Woolridge resigned and, after getting financial backing from Thompson products in Cleveland, went on to form their own company, which they named TRW, after their initials Thompson, Ramo, Woolridge. It became a giant of the space and technology industry, and eventually bigger than Hughes Aircraft itself.

Don't let your personal interests affect the way you view the decision.

Anchoring Drift

The fifth drift in information analysis is Anchoring Drift. If we have no experience in an area, we tend to anchor to the first number we hear. Harold Geneen, the genius who built ITT into an international conglomerate, was often a victim of Anchoring Drift. I had lunch once with the president of one of his companies. He told me that when he first met Geneen, he was asked for a particular statistic about company production. Not wanting to admit he didn't know the right figure, he made an educated guess. After the meeting, he hurriedly checked and found out he was way off on the number. The next time he met with Harold Geneen, he apologized for it. He gave him the correct number and assured him he'd be more accurate in the future. However, once Harold Geneen had heard the first number, the president couldn't move him off it. Every time he met him in the future, Geneen always went back to that original number. He assumed it was correct, because his mind had anchored to that particular number.

I teach real estate agents to use anchoring when they present offers to sellers. Before they get the offer out of the briefcase, they should say this to the seller: "Now, Mr. Seller, I'm well aware you're asking $200,000 for the property, but please understand that it's very unusual for a full price offer to come in. In fact, most offers come in at about 10 percent below the asking price, which means $180,000 is about what we'd expect." This anchors the seller to the $180,000 figure. Then when the agent presents him the offer and he finds that it's for $185,000, it's so much better than the amount to which he anchored, that he's more likely to accept it.

What does all this have to do with anything? Time and time again, I've seen salespeople anchor a buyer to the least expensive model, because they don't want to scare them off. Then they have a terrible time moving him or her up, because they've now anchored the customer to the lower price.

Avoiding Anchoring Drift requires personal discipline. You have to be prepared to accept information that is different from what you believe to be true. You must also be disciplined enough to gather all the information you intend to, before you start drawing conclusions.

Recency Drift

The sixth Information Drift is Recency Drift. We tend to give more emphasis to what has happened to us more recently. That's why the IRS regularly indicts more people in March than any other month of the year. It's why we see a traffic accident and slow down for a few minutes.

In business, it includes the tendency for salespeople to sell the product on which they've been trained most recently. Let's say that you're a manufacturer's representative who sells kitchen equipment to distributors, who turn around and sell your product to restaurants. Even though your distributors are thoroughly familiar with your equipment, you should be going back frequently to hold training classes on it. They are much more likely to sell your product, rather than your competitors, if they have been recently reminded of it.

This is, of course, the reason for point-of-purchase advertising. Manufacturers want to put their name in front of you, as close to your buying decision as they possibly can. Many times I've picked up a product in a store thinking, "Yes, I've heard about this. I hear it's good," only to realize that the only thing I've heard about it is from the maker's advertisements—which is hardly an unbiased source.

Favorability Drift

Seven is Favorability Drift. We all tend to look harder for information that supports our beliefs. We tend to believe what we want to believe. We need to be disciplined enough to seek information that would deny preconceived notions.

Psychologists proved this with a study at a racetrack. They were studying the attitudes of people immediately before they placed a bet, and immediately after they placed a bet. What they found out was that before people placed their bets, they were uptight, anxious, and unsure they were doing the right thing. Yet, once they'd placed the bet, suddenly Favorability Drift took over. Now their mind worked to support the decision they'd made and they had a tendency to want to go back and double the bet before the race started.

The same principle applies when a business executive makes a decision to invest in, say, a surfboard division. In reality, it's a big mistake. It's a very trendy, highly specialized business that should only be run by people who are fanatical surfers. However, the executive never realizes his mistake because his mind is working to reinforce the decision he made.

Have the discipline to look for information that contradicts your beliefs and contradicts decisions you may have made in the past.

Presentation Drift

All of the Information Drifts that we've talked about come into play when we're gathering or analyzing the information ourselves. We have an additional problem if another person is gathering the information for us—because she might be biased in the way she presents the information to us. Presentation Drift puts another spin on the ball, because while she may have compensated for the seven Information Drifts, the information is still inaccurate to us—the problem solver—because of her bias in presenting it.

The four things to look for are:

1. Personal Stake.
2. Expertise.
3. Prejudice.
4. Time pressure.

If you do have someone else gathering the information for you, run down this mental checklist:

> Does the person who's giving me this information have a personal stake in this decision? Is he or she consciously or unconsciously trying to sway my opinion?

> Does the person who's gathering the information have an acceptable amount of expertise in this area? Observations from the uninformed can be dangerous.

> Is the person presenting the information prejudiced? He may not have a personal stake in your decision, but he may have a prejudice. For example, he may be more of a risk taker than you'd be, or less of a risk taker. He may have a prejudice against expanding into different industries, or he may have a prejudice against outsourcing your production to a foreign country.

> How much time did this person have to put the data together? If she accumulated the data under too much time pressure, there's a danger of superficial reporting.

Good problem solvers don't condemn the other person for bias in presenting information. However, they are aware of the four biases, and know how to subtly compensate for Presentation Drift.

▶ Key points from this chapter

Gathering information is critical to good problem solving. However, there are many difficulties attached to gathering information accurately. We tend to drift from accurate analysis, based on the seven Information Drifts covered in this chapter:

▶ Availability Drift: We give more weight to information that is readily available to us. Just because you've heard more about something, doesn't make it more prevalent.

▶ Experience Drift: We give emphasis to things with which we're more familiar.

▶ Conflict Drift: We tend to reject information that doesn't conform to our belief system.

▶ Selectivity Drift: Because we can't absorb everything, we screen out what doesn't interest us.

▶ Anchoring Drift: We tend to form an opinion based on the first number we hear, and give less weight to subsequent input.

▶ Recency Drift: We give more weight to what we've experienced recently.

▶ Favorability Drift: We tend to believe what we want to believe.

When you're relying on someone else to gather information for you, consider the four biases he or she may have:

▶ Does the person who's giving me this information have a personal stake in this decision?

▶ Does the person who's gathering the information, have an acceptable amount of expertise in this area?

▶ Is the person presenting the information prejudiced?

▶ How much time did this person have to put the data together?

Being aware of these Information Drifts will cause you to develop much more accurate information.

Brainstorming

> *The good ideas are all hammered out in agony*
> *by individuals, not spewed out by groups.*

—Charles Brower

Will brainstorming help you solve your problem? Are you better off getting other people involved in the process, or should you be a dynamic leader who goes it alone?

Charles Brower, whom I quoted above, was a brilliant copywriter who became known as Madison Avenue's favorite phrase maker. He was probably referring to advertising slogans, not problem solving. Are there some problems that are better solved autocratically? (The answer is yes, and I'll tell you what they are.) What are the advantages of brainstorming? What are the structured ways of setting up a brainstorming? How many people should be involved in the brainstorming? When does brainstorming create more problems than it solves?

Let's first talk about something that gives managers sleepless nights the world over. First thing in the morning, you can see blurry-eyed executives in the coffee shops of the Hyatts, the Marriotts, and the Sheratons. They're trying to jump-start their brains with black coffee, because they've been up half the night agonizing over this dilemma: "Should I go ahead and make the decision myself, or should I get other people involved in this?"

Here's how the executive vacillates on whether or not to take it to a group decision:

> "If I go ahead and make the decision myself, and I'm as right as I think I am, to what greatness it could lead! Perhaps I'm at the high tide of my career. As Shakespeare said, 'Taken at the flood it would lead to great fortune.' Should I seize this moment, tuck it under my arm like running back Walter Payton, and run for the end zone? If I were right, what a glorious moment it would be! Everyone would hail me as a courageous genius, a bold innovator, a captain of industry; perhaps even a master of the universe.
>
> "On the other hand, what if I'm wrong? Uh oh, then I'm really in trouble. Decades from now they'll hold business classes in campuses across the nation on Dawson's Folly.
>
> "Or worse yet, I could be right, but everyone in the organization gangs up to teach me a lesson. They're all saying I'm a stuck-up, pompous, jackass who needs to be taught a lesson. Because I didn't get them involved in the decision. They'll give lip service to the whole project and I'll be left hanging, twirling slowly in the breeze. Should I get other people involved in solving the problem or shouldn't I?"

In this section we'll examine the good and the bad of brainstorming. The answers will surprise you and you'll learn that there's a lot more to brainstorming than encouraging a group of people to throw out opinions.

Chapter 31

Should You Brainstorm or Not?

We call taking the problem to a group "brainstorming." You can brainstorm with one person, which can be a lot of fun if it's the right person. Or you can brainstorm with 100 people or more, which can be plain awful. We'll talk in a minute about how big the brainstorming group should be.

Let's review the four rules of brainstorming:

1. Encourage a high quantity of ideas by never criticizing any of them.

2. Never reject an idea. Instead add to the idea even if it reverses the impact. For example: One person might say, "Why don't we let the union run it?" Instead of saying, "But then we'd lose control completely," you say, "And we could have a management committee that closely supervises them."

3. Encourage new "off-the-wall" ideas. It adds to the creativity.

4. Encourage everyone to combine the ideas that are brought up.

There are five situations when you should opt for brain-storming rather than making the decision on your own:

1. You think that brainstorming will generate more options.
2. When outside expertise would be helpful.
3. When you want to raise the ethical standards of the way you solve the problem.
4. When you need the support of the group to follow through on solving the problem.
5. When you're afraid the brainstorming group will turn down your way of solving the problem.

Let's take a look at the reasons for each of these:

1. You think that brainstorming will generate more options

When you've done everything you can to gather all the in-formation, and you still don't think you have enough, try brain-storming. It usually generates more options for you because it stimulates creative thought.

2. When outside expertise would be helpful

For example, with an outside board of directors you may have an expert on transportation, international law, or han-dling strikes in Argentina. It's the kind of expertise you sim-ply don't have available to you in your company, and you'd be foolish not to take advantage of it.

3. When you want to raise the ethical standards

That's why a hospital has a surgeon's review board. Any time surgery doesn't go according to plan, the board of sur-geons reviews the case and gives recommendations. One or two people might be willing to cover up malpractice, but the larger the group, the less likely you'll lower the ethical stan-dards of everyone.

Brainstorming usually raises the ethical standards, but don't assume this means that brainstorming a problem will always be more cautious than individuals. Brainstorming will usually be both more cautious than the individual, but also may support less advisable decisions than an individual.

Let's say that a candidate for president is ahead in the polls when he suspects that a major contributor to his or her campaign is not a citizen as he or she was told, even though the contributor has been living in this country for 30 years. That makes it a contribution from a foreign national, which is illegal. But if the candidate returns the money it means pulling a planned advertising campaign in a swing state.

If the candidate must make the decision alone he may well be tempted to think, "I'll ignore it. If the truth comes out I can always claim plausible deniability." If he brainstormed it with his inner circle they would probably advise him to return the money, saying that the cover-up is always worse than admitting a mistake.

However, if he decided to brainstorm the problem with a much larger group they may well recommend ignoring the problem. It would only take a few key members of the group to say, "Let's forget it," and the group would collectively shrug its shoulders and say, "That's fine with me." The opinion of the key people usually sways the opinion of all the other brainstormers. It seems strange but brainstormers will be more cautious, and more reckless, than individuals solving problems alone.

Let's imagine that you were the chief of production at Walt Disney studios. Your company has done fabulously well with cartoon movies and is now branching out into wildlife movies. Your movie, *Wild Wilderness* premiers tomorrow. You have paid for nine different wildlife photographers to spend four years photographing wildlife in Alberta, Canada. The most spectacular sequence, filmed by photographer James

Simon, depicts lemmings apparently committing mass suicide. It seems such a spectacular sequence that it makes your movie a shoe-in for the Academy Award. The sequence will enter the public consciousness and be remembered for decades to come. The expression "like lemmings jumping off a cliff," will enter the English language as a simile for mistakenly following others into a disastrous situation.

Then photographer James Simon tells you, "I need to tell you something. We faked the lemming sequence. They don't fall off cliffs into the ocean. There isn't any ocean in Alberta. Lemmings don't even live in Alberta. We imported them from Hudson Bay and put them on a fake turntable at the top of a riverbank and shot them off. We used trick photography to make it look like there were hundreds of them."

"Lemmings don't commit suicide?" you scream.

"Of course they don't. They migrate if their habitat gets crowded, but that was too boring to film."

If you had brainstormed this with Walt and Roy Disney they probably would have said, "No, we can't risk the credibility of our company for a fake sequence." (We still don't know if Walt knew about this or not. Up until then he had been a good friend to rodents.) If you brainstormed it with all the theater owners they might well say, "If it sells tickets let's run it."

It seems strange but brainstormers can be more reckless than individuals solving problems alone.

The classic example of this was the Bay of Pigs decision. Individually Kennedy's advisors knew it was a mistake to use U.S. troops to support an invasion of Cuba. But they all got swept up with the desire to be a team player. Arthur Schlesinger had stated in writing that he considered the proposed invasion of Cuba immoral. But Robert Kennedy took him aside and said, "You may be right or you may be wrong, but...don't push any further."

4. When you need the support of the group

Unless you just got here from North Korea you're well aware of the value of getting the group involved in the decision. People will simply support decisions with more enthusiasm when they helped make the decision.

However, be careful you're not being manipulative. When I was in my 20s and just getting started up the corporate ladder, I was very much an autocratic decision maker. I knew what was right for the organization, and I didn't see any reason to waste a lot of time getting other people involved in the decision-making process. My boss at the time, Don Rainwater, was much smarter than I. He told me that if I wanted the support of the organization, I had to let them make the decision.

Still, I was young and foolish enough to think I could work my way around that one with no problem. I typed up the six things I wanted to get approved and made enough copies for the group. Then I led them into a discussion on the problem we were having. But I led the discussion so skillfully that they ended up deciding on the same six things. Then with a flourish, I produced the prepared sheet of paper and distributed it to the group saying, "I believe this is what we all agreed upon." They were generous enough to see the humor in this situation, but Don Rainwater took me out to the woodshed and beat me bloody, and rightfully so.

Be persuasive in leading the group to the right decision, but avoid being manipulative. Do it right, and accept input from the rest of the group.

5. When you're afraid the brainstorming group will turn down your idea

That's an absolute. Anytime you're concerned they'd reject your proposal, you must take it to the group.

The problem is, we get so excited about something that we fall in love with our own ideas. For example, we just know we can take the Australian market by storm with this new high tech fly deterrent. It works on batteries, is rechargeable, and will scare off flies for a one hundred foot radius. We can get exclusive distribution rights, and manufacture it in Vietnam lower than anywhere else in the world. With the swarms of flies in Australia, there's no way it's going to fail. However, if I take it to the executive committee for approval, those people are such "sticks in the mud," that they'll never go with it.

Hey, wait a minute! Whom are you trying to kid? If you can't convince the 10 people on your executive committee, what chance do you have of convincing the two thousand people in your organization that it's a good idea? What chance do you have of convincing the 22 million people in Australia that it's great? Come to your senses! If you don't want to take it to the group because you're afraid they'll turn it down, that's exactly when you should be brainstorming.

➡ Key points from this chapter

There are five reasons for brainstorming the problem:

▶ You think that brainstorming will generate more solutions.

▶ When outside expertise would be helpful.

▶ When you want to raise the ethical standards of the decision.

▶ When you need the support of the group to follow through on the solution.

▶ When you're afraid the group will turn down your idea.

Chapter 32

The Advantages of Brainstorming

Now let's talk about the eight advantages of brainstorming versus making a solo decision:

1. Brainstorming catches other people's mistakes.
2. Brainstorming forces action on problems.
3. Brainstorming increases trust in the organization.
4. Brainstormers will reject erroneous information.
5. Brainstorming generates more information.
6. You're going to get more information with which to work.
7. Employees support decisions better when they were involved in the problem-solving process.
8. Brainstorming stops you from doing dumb things.

Let's examine each of these:

Brainstorming catches other people's mistakes.

Try this problem:

A man buys a watch in a store for $65. The watch costs the merchant $30. The man pays with a $100 money order and gets $35 cash back. The money order turns out to be stolen and the merchant can't redeem it. How much is the merchant out?

It's a mind bender isn't it? Individuals get confused on this kind of problem, whereas brainstormers can handle it better because they point out the mistakes of the others.

If you're still working on it, the answer is this: The merchant's out $65 (the $30 cost of the watch plus the $35 cash he gave back to the man).

That's why brainstorming often out-performs individual problem solving.

Brainstorming forces action on problems

Let's face it: Everybody in an organization has his or her own problems. Unless the new computer assembly plant in Sao Paulo directly affects them, they're not going to worry about it too much. To solve that problem try announcing that next week there's going to be a meeting to discuss whether or not to go ahead with the new plant in Brazil. Suddenly, you'll have everyone getting involved in the project. They start accumulating information, and getting background on it, so they can give intelligent input. So, brainstorming forces people to get involved in a project they might otherwise ignore.

Brainstorming increases trust in the organization

When people feel the organization is involving them in problem solving, they trust the organization more. Job satisfaction goes up, along with motivation and morale.

You shouldn't treat employee involvement as a tool to get more support however. Employee involvement should be a leadership philosophy.

Good organizations move from telling their people what to do, to selling them on the solution to the problem, to consulting (getting input from their people), to jointly solving problems with them, and the final step, delegating problem solving.

You should only delegate when you have trained your people how to solve problems and are confident that they are using the same problem-solving methods as you.

Brainstormers will reject erroneous information

Somebody might come to the brainstorming session with a proposal to buy a distribution warehouse in Mobile, Alabama. If they could have made the decision autocratically, they'd have done it by now. Yet, when they present it to the Huddle, somebody who knows that part of the world says, "Wait a minute. Have you checked the union environment in Mobile? That's one of the worst union towns in the country. Don't go ahead before you find out exactly what you're getting into." Brainstorming rejects erroneous information and reveals areas where more research needs to be done.

You're going to get more information with which to work

That's obvious, but it isn't always good news. You can easily get bogged down in too much information. Be careful that inputting too much information doesn't lead to indecisiveness. As a leader you have to be willing to say, "We know enough about the problem. Now let's pick a solution and focus on making that solution work."

The information tends to be more thorough

In plain language that means the people might try to BS one on one. But when they have to present to a brainstorming group, they're going to be much more thorough in their research, and draw conclusions more carefully.

The last two are advantages we've already discussed, but they bear repeating:

> ➧ Employee cooperation. People will move more willingly to support decisions when they took part in the problem-solving process.

187

❯❯ Brainstorming forces you to sell your solution to other people. It stops you from doing dumb things.

❯❯ Key points from this chapter

There are eight advantages to brainstorming.

▶ Brainstorming catches other people's mistakes.

▶ Brainstorming forces action on problems.

▶ The process increases trust in the organization.

▶ Brainstormers will reject erroneous information.

▶ Brainstorming generates more information.

▶ You're going to get more information with which to work.

▶ Employees support decisions better when they were involved in the problem-solving process.

▶ Brainstorming stops you from doing dumb things.

I didn't see it then, but it turned out that getting fired from Apple was the best thing that could have ever happened to me. The heaviness of being successful was replaced by the lightness of being a beginner again, less sure about everything. It freed me to enter one of the most creative periods of my life.

—Steve Jobs

Chapter 33
Structured
Brainstorming

We're all familiar with formal and semi-formal brainstorming. That's the committee meeting, the executive committee, the board of directors, and creative brainstorming. However, there are three other structured methods of brainstorming about which I want to teach you. They're more involved, but they may be very helpful when you're faced with a highly complicated or obscure problem.

Solo brainstorming

That seems like an oxymoron, doesn't it? A contradiction in terms. Like *jumbo shrimp, postal service,* and *normal teenager.*

However, it can be a great problem-solving tool. Here's how it works.

First, take 15 minutes to write down every possibility that occurs to you. Think of yourself as a photographer who takes hundreds of pictures, and later selects the one that's just right. Remember the thousands of pictures that are taken for books in the series *One Day in the Life of a Country*? The threshold theory says: The more you have to choose from, the better the quality.

Then wait until that afternoon or the next morning, and go at it again. Meanwhile, your subconscious mind will have been at work on the problem. Being able to do this over two separate sessions is a big advantage over group brainstorming, which logistically needs to be done at one session. In the meantime, mention the problem to others and get their input.

Next separate your list into an A list and B list. Don't be too selective; include anything that might work on your A list and only put the things you know won't work on to the B list.

Then, rate the ideas on your A list from 1 to 10.

Try pairing the best three ideas on your list with all the other ideas. This random association will usually trigger new possibilities. And finally, take the best idea on your B list, and pair it with all the other ideas.

Analogy brainstorming

This concentrates on looking at the problem from new directions, rather than stimulating a high quantity of creative options.

These are the phases you go through, and the first three are common to all problem-solving processes:

1. Present a detailed statement of the problem to the group.

2. Overload the group with information about the problem. This brings hidden aspects of the problem into the open.

3. Be sure every member of the group thoroughly understands the problem, by asking them to restate it in their words. This is important because in a corporate environment, it's very hard for some people to admit they don't understand what this is all about. They sit there and listen to what's going on, hoping all the pieces will drop into place for them.

To be sure they all understand, you might say to the group, "Okay, let's go around the table. I want each of you to give me a quick statement. Why do you think we're opening up a computer assembly plant in Sao Paulo? I want each of you to come up with a new reason. Don't repeat something that someone's already said."

The first person might say, "Because we can make them cheaper there, than anywhere else."

The second person adds to this: "I thought the major reason is the subsidies the Brazilian government will give us."

The third person might say, "Well, isn't the improved access to the South American market a key consideration, too?" As it goes around the table everybody gets a much clearer understanding of the problem you're facing.

4. Develop analogies, for a better understanding of the problem. An analogy is a figure of speech that attempts to make something clear by comparing it with something else. "As exciting as watching grass grow" is an analogy. So is Tallulah Bankhcad's description of herself: "As pure as driven slush." Analogies are effective in problem solving because they cause the mind to make a great leap in thinking.

There are four types of analogies:
» Direct analogies.
» Personal analogies.
» Fantasy analogies.
» Symbolic analogies.

Perhaps we might have a group of executives discussing a new car at an automobile company. The rule of the game is they need to express their preference as an analogy.

One executive might start with a direct analogy by saying, "The lines should be as smooth as Bailey's Irish Cream." Another might respond with a personal analogy, "I want it to be as exciting as my first toboggan run."

Then somebody chimes in with a fantasy analogy, "It should sparkle like Cinderella's carriage." Yet another might contribute the symbolic analogy: "The acceleration should explode." Analogies are effective in problem solving because they cause the mind to make a great leap in thinking.

Thomas Edison was using an analogy when he said, "I'm experimenting upon an instrument that does for the eye what the phonograph does for the ear." The analogy helped him to apply what he had learned from inventing the phonograph to the invention of the motion picture projector.

Steve Jobs of Apple computers said, "I want Apple TV to do for movie distribution what the iPod did for music distribution."

To begin phase four, ask everybody in the group to come up with an analogy relating to the problem you're facing. They don't have to rotate through the analogies, but I'll do that just to illustrate the difference between the four types.

Direct Analogies. Somebody starts with a direct analogy about the computer assembly plant in Brazil. He or she might say, "Well, the operation should flow like oil through a pipeline."

Somebody else might jokingly respond, "Well, that's a better analogy than sending it on the Exxon Valdez." These analogies might trigger a discussion of pipelines of supplies through Central America during a civil war. Or shipping problems that might exist. The word *pipeline* might even trigger talk of sabotage, and a discussion about security precautions at the plant.

Personal Analogies. Then somebody might use a personal analogy: "The unemployment is so bad there, that for the Brazilians, going to work will be as exciting as going to Disneyland for the first time."

Somebody else might respond, "Well, that's an interesting thought, because we are importing a new type of technology to the country. It's like when Disneyland opened up in Tokyo. They faced all kinds of ethnic considerations that were strange to them."

"I know a consultant that worked with Disney on that project," somebody else might say. "Let me give them a call and see if they know anything about the problems we're facing."

Fantasy Analogies. Next a fantasy analogy may be used: "This is going to seem so strange to the workers. It will seem like *Star Wars* to them."

Somebody might say, "If only we could program them to do the work the way R2-D2 could program itself." From this might be triggered a thought about program systems and employee orientation and training.

Symbolic Analogies. Finally, somebody might use a symbolic analogy: "This should push our profits through the roof." This causes everybody suddenly to visualize the roof of the plant. And somebody says, "Have we considered putting a helicopter pad on the roof of that plant? We have a corporate helicopter at our Rio location, don't we? Wouldn't it make sense to do that?"

In this way, the conversation bounces around the room. Analogy brainstorming groups are small and the people better qualified to come up with solutions. The value of analogy brainstorming is this: It makes the familiar seem strange. Through the analogies you see the problem in a different way. Just beware of reading too much into analogies.

Computer brainstorming

This provides for feedback of individual contributors, the objective assessment of input, opportunities to revise previously stated views, and anonymity for the participants.

There are five phases:

1. Exploration.

2. Interpretation.

3. Reconciliation.

4. Evaluation.

5. Feedback to participants.

It's done with computer surveys; the respondents never meet face to face.

Stage one: Exploration. In this stage you ask each participant to contribute information to the survey. For example, you may run a nationwide chain of fast food restaurants. At your annual meeting in Acapulco the question of adding doughnuts to the line came up. There appeared to be popular support for this, so you'd like to get some more input on it. In the exploration stage, you might send out a memo on your computer network that says this: "At the Acapulco meeting there was support for adding doughnuts to the line. We'd like to get some feedback. Please give me three reasons why you think this is a good idea and three reasons why you think this is a bad idea."

Stage two: Interpretation stage. This is when a group of data processing experts at head office attempts to understand how the participants view the problem—where they agree and where they disagree. It's possible, at this stage, that you'll get such overwhelming support for the program that you'll want to run with it. Or, you get such overwhelming condemnation that you want to drop the idea. If you have significant disagreement, though, you now move on to the next stage.

Stage three: Reconciliation. In the reconciliation stage, the head office team eliminates the more extreme responses. They ignore the 10 percent who loved the plan, and the 10 percent that hated it. From among the more moderate supporters of the plan, they reach for agreement. For example, a follow-up letter might go back out with questions such as "How would you feel if we only offered doughnuts during the morning?" or "What if we only offered doughnuts on a take-out basis?" The response to this questionnaire uncovers the reasons for the difference of opinion.

Stage four: Evaluation. This is when you analyze all the information and condense it into options for a management decision. The head office team may report: "There's very little support for carrying doughnuts throughout the day. The feeling is it would cut into lunch and dinner sales. However, 82% of the managers like the idea for the morning hours. They're less agreed on whether it should only be a take out item. 57% think they should only be available at the drive up. 43% think it would increase add-on sales, if they were also available inside."

Stage five: Summarization. Here you feed the information back to the participants, in a summarized form. This gives them a better idea of why management arrived at the final decision. It draws in the support of people who may have opposed it, or favored a different version of the same basic decision. Or people who may have favored a less modified version of the original decision.

The advantages of computer huddling are these:

» You can involve more people than is practical in a face-to-face brainstorming session.

» It's cheaper than getting them together.

» Severe disagreement can be more easily resolved, because of the anonymity of the people involved in the survey.

» Dominant personalities can't sway the opinions of the other participants.

➡ Key points from this chapter

▶ Not all brainstorming involves getting a group of people to a meeting and having them contribute solutions to the problem.

▶ Solo brainstorming has the advantage of being easy to do. It is not labor-intensive. Rapidly make a list of possible solutions. Don't screen them at this point. As with group brainstorming there are no bad ideas at this early stage. Separate the list into A and B solutions, and let simmer for a few hours. Try pairing solutions.

▶ Analogy brainstorming is valuable because it causes the imagination to fly.

▶ Computer brainstorming allows for a great number of people to input their reactions to solutions anonymously.

Section Eight

What Makes You a Great Problem Solver?

I have only one yardstick by which I test every
major problem — and that yardstick is:
Is it good for America?

—Dwight D. Eisenhower

By now you should feel much better about your problem-solving ability.

▶ Great problem solvers can act quickly and decisively, but they don't let people force them into making decisions under time pressure.

▶ Great problem solvers understand the need to gather information, and work through the problem-solving process. But if speed is essential, they're willing to move with less than all the facts they'd like to have.

▶ Great problem solvers become completely committed to their decisions, and yet they're always willing to pull the plug if it turns out they made a mistake.

▶ Great problem solvers are bold and courageous in their decisions, but know they mustn't be too autocratic.

In our final chapter, let's examine the traits of great problem solvers.

Chapter 34
Traits of Great Problem Solvers

To complete your lessons in problem solving, in this chapter I'll teach you the seven traits that make you a great problem solver. They are:

1. Having a high tolerance for ambiguity.
2. Moving from where the problem is hurting you.
3. Being a good listener.
4. Always building consensus around a decision.
5. Avoiding stereotypes.
6. Being realistic about the cost and difficulty.
7. Avoiding experts who tell you it won't work.

The first trait: Having a high tolerance for ambiguity

Good problem solvers have a high tolerance for ambiguity. They don't have to have everything laid out in black and white for them. They don't have to know every little detail that's going on. They may be aware there are problems in the plant in Bangkok, but they're comfortable with the framework they've set up. They know somehow it'll get taken care of, because they don't have to be there for problems to get resolved. Most of us either feel comfortable with this kind of ambiguity, or we don't.

I used to have a low tolerance for ambiguity. I didn't like to travel unless every flight and hotel room and rental car had been booked and confirmed. I decided to break myself of this habit by travelling around the world without preplanning anything.

I simply bought a "round the world" air ticket, and took off for five weeks, following the sunset. I could go anywhere I wanted, as long as I kept going west and never backtracked. Without any plans or hotel reservations, I went to Tahiti, New Zealand, Australia, Singapore, and Thailand. Then I flew to Frankfurt, Germany, where I rented a car and drove around Europe for a couple of weeks. I finally picked up a flight in Paris for the trip back across the Atlantic. It was the most exciting, enriching vacation I've ever taken.

Now I don't have a problem with taking a trip like that, where nothing is planned ahead. Had I spent a month planning the trip, I'd have run into less frustration and maybe seen more. But would it have been as much fun? I don't think so.

I thought it was such a great idea, that when my youngest son, John, graduated from college, I gave him a similar trip. I went with him for the first three weeks. We rented a car and drove around Japan for 10 days, nearly getting to the top of Mount Fuji, even though it wasn't the climbing season, and we didn't have our climbing gear with us. Then we flew to Seoul, Korea where we'd heard that students were staging a massive government protest. We actually got to be on the front line with the leader of the government riot police as they donned gas masks and prepared to fight the students. Next we rented a car in Taipei and drove around the island of Taiwan for a week, with a side trip to do some white-water rafting. Finally we flew to Hong Kong, where I left him and returned to California. He continued on around the world, trying to stretch his spending money as far as he could. He stayed with friends in New Delhi, and then flew down to the Maldives for some scuba diving. Next he flew to the south of France and ended up spending several weeks with friends in Paris. I didn't see him again until I decided to spend some time with my first wife's relatives in Iceland, and he flew up from Paris to be with me. Finally, he completed his round-the-world pilgrimage, having been gone for more than four months. Not once on this trip did he pre-book a hotel room. Sure, for the same amount of money I could have bought him a car, or put a down payment on a home, but where's the fun in that? He not only had a great time, but he learned a wonderful lesson: the ability to live with ambiguity.

Some people wouldn't dream of doing something like that, because they have a low tolerance for ambiguity. They want to have everything planned in advance; they don't want to leave anything to chance.

That's a very good characteristic to have when you're dealing with a problem that is not urgent and you can take your time deciding what to do. It's a terrible characteristic to have when the crunch is on, and you have to solve the problem now or your world will collapse around you. You probably invested in this book to learn how make the right choice when faced with a problem. But the right choice isn't always the perfect solution. Almost invariably, you'll have to go ahead with something that only has a good chance of succeeding but no guarantees. If you have a low tolerance for ambiguity, this will drive you crazy.

The second trait: Moving from where the problem is hurting you

If you're in psychological, physical, or financial pain over a problem, you must learn to move away from the place where the problem is hurting you, before you try to solve it.

You can't see the big picture when you're standing in the middle of it. As the saying goes, "When you're up to your elbows in alligators, it's hard to remember that your initial objective was to drain the swamp."

If people would see the value of moving away from the problem in their personal lives, they would become big believers in it when it came to corporate problem solving. Some people stay in unhappy marriages for year after year after year. They never have the courage to say, "I need to move away from this in order to view it objectively. It doesn't really matter where I go, but I want to move away from this situation and take another look at it from over there."

It's amazing how often, when you get over there, the situation isn't nearly as hopeless as it was when you were in the middle of it. You really do have a lot more options than you think you do.

Let's say that you have spent a whole week planning the perfect picnic with someone you love. You want everything to be just right, because at the appropriate moment you're going to pull a diamond ring out of your pocket and propose. It's a perfect day and you've laid out your tablecloth in the middle of a meadow. The sky is blue and the birds are singing. Just as you're about to make your move, a dam breaks upstream and a 10-foot wall of water rushes down the valley toward you.

You can make a very good point that it isn't fair. You can make a very good case that it shouldn't happen to you. You might say to yourself, "God is trying to tell me something," and quickly slip the ring back in your pocket.

You can choose any one of these reactions, but the point is: Do it over there. Don't try to solve problems in the middle of the meadow where you're going to get hurt by the problem. Move to where you're not being hurt, and then do all the complaining you want.

Some parents agonize for years over a problem teenager. It's driving them to the brink of insanity. They can't decide what to do. If they would just learn to move away from the problem, they would learn how, magically, the problem can be solved much more easily. Now, in this case, it's the problem teenager who has to do the moving. But once you've taken the initiative and thrown him out of the house, probably you'll be saying to yourself, "Why didn't I do this years ago?" In all probability, it will cause the teen to get his or her act together. Almost without a doubt, he or she will still love you just as much, if not more than before. There's every probability it will improve the relationship between you. The third rule for seeing the big picture is to do your seeing from somewhere else rather than in the middle of the problem.

The third trait: Being a good listener

I can guarantee you that if you take two business executives and one is a good listener and one is a bad listener, the one who's a good listener will always be the better problem solver. It's especially critical in this day and age when we're bombarded with information. A top executive may spend 80 percent of his or her time in meetings listening to discussions. It's very frustrating, it's often very boring, and unless we're an expert listener we won't get from the discussion what we need to make a good choice. Let's talk about improving our listening skills in three different areas:

1. Increasing your concentration so your mind doesn't wander while you're listening.

2. Increasing your comprehension of what's said.

3. Improving your ability to evaluate what's said.

Increasing your concentration. Our mind quickly wanders when the speaker is boring, but our reactions can encourage a more interesting presentation. Here are some positive things you can do for the speaker:

➡ Lean forward.

➡ Tilt your head a little to show you're paying attention.

➡ Ask questions.

➡ Give feedback.

➡ Mirror what he or she said.

If you think of listening as an interactive process, you do much better.

Next, avoid boredom by playing mind games. Concentrate on what's he or she's saying, not the style of delivery. You can do this by picking the longest word in a sentence or rephrasing what just been said. Because you can listen four times faster than the speaker can speak, you need to do something or your mind will wander.

You can raise your alertness level by changing your breathing pattern. If you want to become more alert, breathe in more than you breathe out. This feeds oxygen to the brain. Breathe in to a six count and out to a three count. Sounds stupid, doesn't it? But it works. It works in reverse to relieve stress. Under stress, breathe in to a three count and out to a six count. It's amazing how this relaxes you.

Increasing your comprehension. First, take notes right from the start of the conversation. Whether it's one on one, in a committee meeting, or you're in the audience at a large meeting. Take a large pad of paper with you. Head it up with the date and the topic, and start to keep brief notes on what's being said. Paper is cheaper than the time it takes to go back and get the details. Perhaps you take notes like this, but there's no reason for any follow up, so you throw them away. But chances are, you'll file it somewhere and it becomes a very valuable resource for you. Also, of course, it communicates to the other person that you care about what he or she is saying. An additional bonus is that when people see you're writing things down, they tend to be a lot more accurate in what they're telling you.

Next, defer making judgment about the speaker until he or she is through. If you immediately analyze someone as phony or manipulative or self-serving, you tend to shut him or her out and quit listening. Just hold off, and wait until he or she is through, before you evaluate.

Ask questions if it's possible. This is a creative interruption.

Now here's a key point in increasing comprehension: Know in advance what you're listening for. If you sit in an audience and just listen to a speaker, there's a very good chance your mind will wander during much of the talk, unless he's a particularly skilled speaker. However, if you go to the talk saying to yourself, "I want to learn what this man has to say about a particular issue," you'll be much more focused in what you bring away from it.

Next, recognize which side of the brain is dominating. If you feel angry or excited by something you hear, which is a right-brain reaction, switch left by concentrating on facts and figures. If you feel bored or impatient by what's said, which is left-brain thinking, switch right by putting yourself in the shoes of the speaker and empathizing with his or her feelings.

The second thing that improves your evaluation of what they're saying is to be aware of your personal biases. Be conscious of how they're coloring your reactions. For example, if you're aware that you don't like attorneys, you're aware that this is causing you to distrust the person who's talking to you. You can evaluate the information much more clearly when you're aware of your biases. Perhaps you're a person who can't stand people trying to hype you, and you tend to resist what they have to say whether it's right or whether it's wrong. Be aware of that. It improves your ability to evaluate what they're saying.

Don't let your enthusiasm for a concept carry you away. Sometimes you start to listen to people and it sounds so great, you can't wait to implement it. You're usually better off to train yourself to listen to all the facts, before you jump on the bandwagon. Not only may a fact come to light that cools you on the idea, a fact may appear that makes you even more enthusiastic, because it triggers a thought that would improve the concept.

Finally, learn to take notes with a divided note pad, one with a line down the middle. On the left you list the facts as they were presented, on the right you note your evaluation of what was said.

The fourth trait: Always building consensus around a solution

Great problem solvers pick a solution they know will have the support of the people, and follow through to be sure they get that support.

Remember the dog food story that has been circulating in business for years? A major company spent years researching a new line of dog food. They spent millions of dollars on an advertising campaign, but the dog food didn't sell. The president of the company called in all the salespeople and said, "Why aren't you doing your job? What's gone wrong here? We spent millions on market research. We spent millions of dollars on advertising. Why can't you sell it?" Somebody in the back of the room said, "You forgot to ask the dogs if they liked it!"

Be sure you're *asking the dogs* before you go ahead and make the final decision!

The other aspect of building consensus around a decision is being sure you have the support of the people who must implement the program. I know you're such a brilliant motivator that you can get anybody to do anything; I understand that! But wouldn't it be a lot easier to ride the horse the way it's going? However tempting the decision may be, if you don't have the enthusiastic support of the people who must implement it, say no. As I said earlier, ride the horse the way it's going, and if it drops dead, get off fast.

Some smart people have made this mistake. I remember talking to a Wall Street financier who'd just purchased one of the smaller national real estate franchises.

"Have your ever been involved in real estate brokerage before?" I asked him. He hadn't, so my next question was: "Then why are you doing this?" It turned out he was already into insurance and mortgage banking. Now he was drooling at the thought of thousands of real estate agents, who were certain to send him insurance and mortgage business. There was a major flaw in the plan: He hadn't asked these agents how they felt about doing that for the owner of the franchise. The answer was that because they were independent contractors, not employees, they could not be forced into sending him their insurance and mortgage business. His plan was a disaster, and two years later he was out of the business, having just taken a multi-million-dollar seminar in problem solving.

The federal government wouldn't have a deficit if it learned this. There are 27 cities in the greater Los Angeles area, and most of them have their own public transportation system. You see these buses running around all over the place with the name of the city on its side. Most of them are running around completely empty. Why would that be? What's going on? They're running around empty because the federal government, in its wisdom, decided it would subsidize these systems to the tune of 90 percent.

No wonder those buses are running around empty. The federal government didn't build a consensus around the decision. They didn't find out if the buses would really have the support of the people who'd use them.

Good problem solvers always build consensus around the decision. Before they go ahead, they're sure they have the support of the people who will use the product or the service. They remember to ask the dogs if they like it. They're sure they have the support of the people who'll implement the plan.

The fifth trait: Avoiding stereotypes

We're all guilty of assumptions, which is a nicer word than prejudice, but means the same thing.

I don't think I have to hammer this point home, but we have to avoid visual stereotyping. Not all men with long hair are hippies. Not all people who wear pocket protectors are nerds. Not all football players are freewheeling in their lifestyle. Not all accountants are boring.

Stereotyping happens because the mind always seeks the shortest route to a decision—the path of least resistance. It's easier to assume that this person or situation fits the mold of your previous experience, rather than to evaluate each person or situation on its merits.

We stereotype in areas we dislike or don't interest us. I don't like English cars, so I tend to lump them together as difficult and expensive to fix. I'm not interested in basketball, so I lump all games and all players together in my mind.

Stereotyping can be valuable because it enables us to draw conclusions even when we have incomplete information. However, it stops us from seeing new combinations of elements in the problem.

We all remember the old riddle about the young man brought to the hospital emergency room. The surgeon says, "I can't treat him, because he's my son." But the young man keeps insisting that his father isn't a doctor; he's an attorney. What's going on? Stereotyping prevents us from seeing the surgeon may indeed be a woman not a man. The answer to the riddle is that the doctor is the patient's mother.

However, worse than any of these stereotypes is an assumption that you can make about yourself: "I am the way I am." Most people at some point in their life congeal. With some people it's 10 years old, with other people it's 100 years old, but at some point in our lives we congeal. We arrive at a point from which we'll never change. Edward R. Morrow said, "Some people haven't had a new thought in years. They've simply been having the same thought over and over."

Don't congeal; you can change the way you are. I know this is true because every month I talk to dozens of Nightingale-Conant customers who validate this. Simply by slipping an audio CD into your car player and letting it play, you can change. Stereotyping other people is disgraceful; stereotyping yourself is tragic.

The sixth trait: Being realistic about the cost and difficulty

This is particularly true when other people are bringing you the idea, asking for your approval. In that situation, most people are over-optimistic. They're enthusiastic about the plan and concerned you might say no. This means they're not realistic about the time and money it's going to take.

Here's my advice, gleaned from starting up some half-dozen different companies. It will cost you at least 20 percent more than you think and probably twice as much. Also, it will take you at least 20 percent longer than you think and maybe twice as long. Say to yourself, "What if this costs me twice as much as I've budgeted, and takes twice as long to get into the black as I think? Is it still a good idea?" If you can answer positively to that, you've probably got an excellent idea on your hands.

Hold everything if your response is a resounding "No way would I go ahead, if it's going to take twice as long and cost twice as much!" You need to take another look at the decision and be more cautious.

Next, be realistic enough to avoid blind trust. Before you go ahead with the decision ask yourself, "Can I adequately supervise the person who'll implement the plan? Or will he be out there somewhere doing whatever he wants?" A way to avoid blind trust is to be sure the person running the plan has just as much to lose as you do. Say to yourself, "A year from now, if this thing has gone down the tubes, what will I have lost?" Compare this to what the person who's pushing this plan will have lost. This doesn't mean he or she has to put cash into the plan. Perhaps she'd have worked for a year without pay, or for substantially less than she could have earned otherwise. Then, she'd also have suffered, so it reduces the risk of the decision. Don't go along with a decision where you'd have lost everything and she'd have lost nothing. She would have had a good job for a year, plus a shot at greatness. All you've done is expose yourself to serious risk.

The seventh trait: Avoiding experts who tell you it won't work

Problem-solving minefields are those areas into which you walk where you have to say to yourself, "I'm walking through a serious minefield here. It may not blow me up, but I need to be very alert." There are five that can really blow up on you:

- If Warren Buffett is investing in it, it must be a steal.
- If they're advertising it, it must be selling.
- If Apple is doing it, it must be right.
- If the person pushing the plan is enthusiastic, he must be able to make it work.
- Experts are telling you it won't work.

If Warren Buffett is investing in it, it must be a steal.

Just because a shrewd businessperson is going ahead, it doesn't follow that it would be a good idea for you. Smart businesspeople make big mistakes, too. But even more important, you and they are probably in completely different situations. It may be a terrific idea for them, and a lousy idea for you. You're walking through a minefield when you make decisions based on what other people do, however smart they may be.

If Apple is doing it, it must be right.

I'm a big fan of Apple products and they have a remarkable history of introducing successful products. But they are not always right.

The first Macintosh portable was a disaster. It weighed a monstrous 15.8 pounds and sold for a massive $6,500. It never got off the ground.

The Apple Newton sounded like a good idea when it was launched. It was the first PDA (Personal Digital Assistant). It could fax messages, could send e-mail, and was designed to read and recognize handwritten notes and designs. It was priced at a massive $1,000, which is almost $1,500 in today's dollars. It was quickly cancelled.

Let's not forget that Apple's profit is more than $4 billion a quarter. With that kind of income you can afford to make a few mistakes.

If the person pushing the idea seems enthusiastic, he must be able to make it work.

Robert Bernstein, chairman of Random House Publishers, says, "Beware of the articulate incompetent. Particularly in a business that depends on people and not machinery. Only intuition can protect you from this most dangerous individual of all."

If the person making the proposal is enthusiastic, it colors the decision-making process. Paul Schoemaker did a study with his students at the University of Chicago Graduate Business School. He presented a business situation and a possible solution to two groups. He told one group the idea had an 80 percent chance of success. He told the other group it had a 20 percent chance of failure. The first group rallied behind the plan. The second group vetoed it.

Minefield number four is: Beware the articulate incompetent. Just because the person pushing the plan is enthusiastic, it doesn't mean they can make it work.

Experts are telling you it won't work.

Experts can be wrong and very frequently are. Twenty-one publishers rejected the book *M*A*S*H*. It became an incredible best-seller, and was turned into a blockbuster movie, followed by a television series that ran for years.

Eighteen publishers rejected *Jonathan Livingston Seagull*, which became the third-best-selling book ever written.

The Munich Technical Institute rejected Albert Einstein because he showed, as they said, "no promise."

And Darryl F. Zanuck wouldn't sign Clark Gable because his ears were too big.

You're walking through a minefield when the experts say it won't work. But you also may be in a minefield when the experts say they're sure it *will* work.

Jonas Salk wouldn't have discovered the cure for polio if he hadn't questioned the experts, who all said that the only way you become immune to a virus disease is to be infected by it. He had the courage to question this, and produced the cure for polio; a disease so dreaded that being inoculated for it had seemed unthinkable. Most great discoveries in science occurred when somebody had the courage to challenge the experts.

And finally, my favorite **"experts say they're sure"** story:

In 1906, astronomer Percival Lowell charted the red canals of the planet Mars so accurately that they were published in maps and schoolbooks throughout the world. Later we found out there are no red canals on Mars. Percival Lowell was suffering from a rare eye disease that caused him to see the veins in his own eyes! But don't fret for him, because he didn't sink into oblivion. The disease is now known throughout the world as Lowell's syndrome.

➠ Key points from this chapter

Remember the seven traits that make you a great problem solver.

▶ Having a high tolerance for ambiguity.

▶ Moving from where the problem is hurting you.

▶ Being a good listener.

▶ Always building consensus around the solution.

▶ Avoiding stereotypes.

▶ Being realistic about the cost and difficulty.

▶ Avoiding experts who tell you it won't work.

Index

Noise, mental, 119-120
Nordstrom, 47
Obama, Barack, 60
Occam's Razor, 35-38
On Anger, 43
Open-ended questions, 159
Overreacting, 15, 53
Pasteur, Luis, 105
Payroll, 24-26
People problems, 11-13, 14-23
Perkins, Dr., 119
Perrier, 90
Personal analogies, 191-192
Personal investment, 84-85
Petersen, Don, 162
Post-it, 105
Prejudice, 173, 174
Presentation Drift, 173
Principle of Parsimony, the, 36
Principle of Plurality, the, 36
Principles, 46-50
Principles, concrete, 87-88
Prioritizing bills, 28-29
Problems, defining, 20-21, 60-63
Problems, imagined, 53-54
Problems, money, 11-13, 24-32
Problems, people, 11-13, 14-23
Problems, real, 53-54
Problems, unique, 57-58
Quantified Evaluation, 143, 147-148
Questions, open-ended, 159
Quickly, acting too, 64-78
Ramo, Dr. Simon, 170

Rating system, 149-151
Reagan, Ronald, 125-126
Real problems, 53-54
Realism, 208
Recency Drift, 166, 172
Reductionism, 98-99
Reno, Janet, 56
Reversibility, 80
Right brain, 109-111, 113-116, 120
Role models, 131-132
Salk, Jonas, 211
Secrets of Power Negotiation, 55
Selectivity Drift, 166, 169-170
Seneca, 42-43, 45
Short-term memory, 102, 108
Smith, C.R., 89
Smith, Fred, 124, 135
Solo brainstorming, 189-190
Solutions, 35-38
Spiritual intuition, 94
Stereotypes, 206-207
Stew Leonard's, 47
Stress, 64, 69, 109-110
Structured brainstorming, 189-190
Subconscious, 109, 145
Sullenberger, "Sulley," 78-80
Summey, Mike, 79
Symbolic analogies, 191-192
Time pressure, 64-69, 160-161, 173, 174
Timing, decision making and, 76-81

About the Author

Roger Dawson was born in England, migrated to California in 1962 and became a United States citizen 10 years later. Formerly the president of one of California's largest real estate companies, he became a full-time author and professional speaker in 1982.

His Nightingale-Conant audio program, *Secrets of Power Negotiating,* is the largest-selling business audio program ever published. Several of his books have been main selections of major book clubs. He is the founder of The Power Negotiating Institute, a California-based organization.

Companies and associations call on him for his expertise in negotiation, persuasion, and decision-making.

He was inducted into the Speaker Hall of Fame in 1991. His seminar company conducts seminars on Power Negotiating, Power Persuasion, Confident Decision Making, and High Achievement throughout the country and around the world.

The Power Negotiating Institute

1045 East Road

La Habra Heights, California 90631 USA

Tel.: 800 YDAWSON [932–9766] from the USA or Canada only

International telephone number 1 (562) 697–7251.

For more information see his Website: *www.RogerDawson.com*

You are welcome to e-mail comments, questions, complaints, and suggestions to Roger@RogerDawson.com.

Also by Roger Dawson

Books

Secrets of Power Negotiating
Secrets of Power Persuasion
Secrets of Power Negotiating for Salespeople
Secrets of Power Persuasion for Salespeople
The 13 Secrets of Power Performance
With Mike Summey: *The Weekend Millionaire series*

Audio Programs

Secrets of Power Negotiating
Secrets of Power Persuasion
Secrets of Power Performance
Confident Decision Making
The Personality of Achievers
Secrets of Power Negotiating for Salespeople

Video Training Programs

Guide to Everyday Negotiating
Guide to Business Negotiating
Guide to Advanced Negotiating Power
Negotiating for Salespeople (a 12-part series)

Speeches and Seminars

If you hire speakers for your company or influence the selection of speakers at your association, you should learn more about Roger Dawson's speeches and seminars. He will customize his presentation to your company or industry so that you get a unique presentation tailored to your needs. You can also arrange to audio or videotape the presentation for use as a continuous training resource.

Roger Dawson's Presentations Include:

Secrets of Power Negotiating
Secrets of Power Persuasion
Secrets of Power Problem Solving
The 13 Secrets of Power Performance

To get more information and receive a complimentary press kit, please call, write, e-mail, or fax to:

The Power Negotiating Institute
1045 East Road
La Habra Heights, CA 90631 USA
Phone: (800) YDAWSON (932–9766)
Fax: (562) 697-1397
E-mail: Roger@RogerDawson.com
Website: http://RogerDawson.com

Here's a listing of Roger Dawson's audio and video programs you can order from the above address and phone number.

Audio CD Programs

Secrets of Power Negotiating $69.95

Six hours of great training on 6 audio CDs. This is one of the largest-selling business audio programs ever published, with sales of over $38 million. You'll learn 20 negotiating gambits that are sure-fire winners. Going beyond the mere mechanics of the power negotiating process, Roger Dawson helps you learn what influences people, and how to recognize and adjust to different negotiating styles, so you can get what you want regardless of the situation.

Also, you'll learn:

➧ A new way of pressuring people without confrontation.

➧ The one unconscious decision you must never make in a negotiation.

➧ The five standards by which every negotiation should be judged.

➧ Why saying yes too soon is always a mistake.

➧ How to gather the information you need without the other side knowing.

➧ The three stages terrorist negotiators use to defuse crisis situations, and much, much more.

Power Negotiating for Salespeople $69.95

Six hours of great training on 6 audio CDs. This program that supplements and enhances Roger Dawson's famous generic negotiating program *Secrets of Power Negotiating,* teaches salespeople how to negotiate with buyers and get higher prices without having to give away extras like freight and extended payment terms. It's the most in-depth program ever created for selling at higher prices than your competition and still maintaining long-term relationships with your customers. It's guaranteed to dramatically improve your profit margins or we'll give your money back.

Special Offer

Invest in both *Secrets of Power Negotiating* and
Power Negotiating for Salespeople and save $30.
Both for only $110.

Secrets of Power Persuasion $69.95

Six hours of great training on 6 audio CDs. In this program, Roger Dawson shows you the strategies and tactics that will enable you to persuade people in virtually any situation. Not by using threats or phony promises, but because they perceive that it's in their best interest to do what you say. You'll learn:

➧ Why credibility and above all, consistency are the cornerstones of getting what you want.

➧ Verbal persuasion techniques that defuse resistance and demonstrate the validity of your thinking.

➧ To develop an overwhelming aura of personal *charisma* that will naturally cause people to like you, respect you, and gladly agree with you.

It's just a matter of mastering the specific, practical behavioral techniques that Roger Dawson presents in a highly entertaining manner.

Secrets of Power Performance $69.95

Six hours of great training on 6 audio CDs. With this program, you'll learn how to get the best from yourself and those around you! Roger Dawson believes that we are all capable of doing more than we think we're capable of. Isn't that true for you? Aren't you doing far more now than you thought you could do five years ago? With the life-changing secrets revealed in this best selling program, you'll be able to transform your world in the next five years!

Confident Decision Making $69.95

Six hours of great training on 6 audio CDs. Decisions are the building blocks of your life. The decisions you've made have given you everything you now have. The decisions you'll make from this point on will be responsible for everything that happens to you for the rest of your life. Wouldn't it be wonderful to know that, from this point on, you'll always be making the right choice? All you have to do is listen to this landmark program.

You'll learn how to:

➧ Quickly and accurately categorize your decision.

➧ Expand your options with a 10-step creative thinking process.

➧ Find the right answer with reaction tables and decision trees.

➧ Harness the power of synergism with the principle of huddling.

➧ Know exactly what and how your boss, customer, or employee will decide, and dozens more powerful techniques.

Order by calling 800 YDAWSON [932–9766]

The toll free number works from the USA or Canada only.

International telephone number 1 (562) 697–7251.

For more information see our Website: www.RogerDawson.com.

Video Training Programs

Guide to Business Negotiations	*One hour DVD video*	*$55*
Guide to Everyday Negotiations	*One hour DVD video*	*$55*
Guide to Advance Negotiations	*One hour DVD video*	*$55*

If you're in any way responsible for training or supervising other people, these videos will liven up your staff meetings and turn your people into master negotiators. Your sales and profits will soar, as you build new win-win relationships with your customers. Then use these programs to develop a training library for your employees' review, and for training new hires.

12-Part Sales Negotiating Video Series $499

Think how your sales and your profit margins would soar, if you could have Roger Dawson speak at your sales meetings once a month! Now you can, with this new series of twelve 30-minute videotapes designed just for this purpose. Dawson goes one-on-one with your salespeople to show them how to out-negotiate your buyers. Play one a month at your sales meetings and watch your people become masterful negotiators!

Special Prices for Career Press readers. Mention this book when you place your order and receive a 20-percent discount on audio or video programs. All major credit cards accepted.

Order by calling 800 YDAWSON [932–9766].

The toll free number works from the USA or Canada only.

International telephone number 1 (562) 697–7251.

For more information see our website: www.RogerDawson.com